Youth Master of Business Administration Series

Marketing

A learning workbook series for junior high and high school students.

Visit the Y.M.B.A. website at www.YMBAgroup.com

ISBN-13: 978-1725196759
ISBN-10: 1725196751

Printed by CreateSpace, An Amazon.com Company.
Available from Amazon.com and other retail outlets.
CreateSpace, Charleston, SC

Copyright protected © 2014, 2018, 2020
All rights reserved.
This workbook publication, or any part of this book, may not be reproduced, distributed, stored in a retrieval system or transmitted in any form for any purpose without prior written approval from the author.

Consult a professional when seeking business advice and decisions. This is a learning book discussing topics in a general style, not intended to be considered professional advice, suggestions or guidance.

Submit all inquiries at the website www.YMBAgroup.com

Y.M.B.A. Marketing - grades 6 7 8 9 10 +   ages 12 13 14 15 16 +

Marketing

We hope to hear from you!

We value your suggestions.

Positive feedback, shares and word of mouth appreciated.

Suggestions, Comments, Questions

always welcome at

www.YMBAgroup.com

THE Y.M.B.A. GROUP - MARKETING
Marketing, Markets and Advertising

TABLE OF CONTENTS

How To Use This Learning Workbook	7
What Is Marketing	8
Product Marketing	14
Feature Marketing	18
The Four "P's"	24
Marketplace Selling	34
AIDA Is Here To Help	36
Follow The Data	38
Goods and Services	42
Wholesale Customers	48
Target Markets	50
Commercial TV	52
Marketing Math	54
Marketing Review Quiz	61
Answer Key	67
Drawing Board Workbook Pages Answer Key	68
Completion Certificate	69

Do you have a suggestion for a book topic?

Let us know and it may be our next book!

www.YMBAgroup.com

How To Use This Book

Thank you for choosing the Y.M.B.A. learning workbook series. I am excited to share the topics with you. As a teacher, corporate professional, M.B.A. and parent, I sought to find a quality program for my children that was both at an introductory level and interesting for their age. When I discovered nothing like this existed, Y.M.B.A. began. A business learning program for young students created and designed by an M.B.A, teacher, and parent. Y.M.B.A. presents information in clear, easy to follow style; focused on students approximately 12 to 16 years of age. I designed the lessons as a combination textbook and workbook because students retain far more when applying the newly taught ideas. The series instructs one idea at a time in a straightforward and simple to understand format. While presenting students with a concept they develop their understanding with fun, level-appropriate examples. After each lesson page is a worksheet to apply the idea from the page prior. This pattern keeps students engaged and actively learning with on-going student applications. The "The Drawing Board" worksheets reinforce the lesson as students practice reasoning, computation, or analysis. Y.M.B.A. focuses on useful business and everyday topics found across industries and in daily life.

Each learning workbook has a quiz for a student demonstration of their new understanding of the subject. As the student completes the learning workbook you will likely see an increase in both pride and confidence. Why wait for business concepts to be introduced? Students are ready to learn about practical life and business topics today. Y.M.B.A. lessons include relevant examples based on familiar student scenarios to sustain learning that is both effective and fun!

Business skills are useful in every industry; an understanding of business is essential. Students can begin achieving more with Y.M.B.A. today and build a path for the future. Your support is appreciated. Suggestions, questions, or comments are always welcome.

Thank you,

L.J. Keller

The quantity of each skill practice area is shown below each learning tile.
Worksheet pages seek to capture student interest and build learning momentum.

What Is Marketing?

Have you watched a commercial on television? Read a billboard? Listened to a radio commercial? Or maybe you have glanced at a flyer? Used a coupon? Or did you ever buy something on sale? Each of these is an example of marketing, and there are many more around you each day!

Marketing describes the steps taken by a business to find buyers. Marketing hopes to motivate buyers to purchase a product or service.

> ***Marketing is the study of the interactions and motivations between customers and sellers buying and selling different goods and services in a market.***

Businesses are known as SELLERS.
Buyers are shoppers are known as CUSTOMERS.
Places to buy are known as a MARKET.
Purchases you can touch are known as GOODS.
People doing a task or offering a skill is known as a SERVICE.
Goods and Services together are known as PRODUCTS.

(SELLERS) bring (PRODUCTS) to the (MARKET) bought by (CUSTOMERS)

What Is The Goal?

A new product begins when a person has an idea. A new business owner believes consumers will enjoy the good or service so they begin marketing. The goal of marketing is to let customers know about the good or service. But did you know just telling customers a product exists is often not enough. Marketing is needed to encourage the shopper to buy.

What are some marketing goals?

To tell of a limited time promotion.
To explain new product features.
To show the benefit of a good or service.
To demonstrate how a product is helpful.

INVESTIGATE

Think of a commercial you recently heard on the radio or watched on TV.

Did the commercial tell ....
how the product was helpful?
Were there .... new features?
Was it .... a limited time sale?

The product I thought of was:

_____

The goal of the commercial was:

_____

The Drawing Board

Invent A Product

Imagine you are an inventor.

A friend challenges you to make a new product. The only materials you may use are:

    screws   glue   fabric

    wood   wheels   paper

You may use as much or as little of each of these materials as you choose. You may also decide to use only some of the materials. You will create your new product in a workshop that has all the tools you need.

Invention Front View

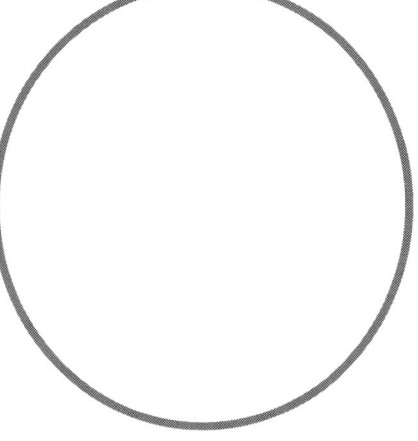

Invention Top View

Invention Back View

Consider the following questions:

1. What did you name your invention? _____

2. What does your invention do? What are the benefits? _____
_____

3. What consumers do you think will buy your invention? _____

4. Will the marketing of the invention focus on a product benefit, a product feature or a limited time sale? _____

EXPLORE

The Marketing Goal

Marketing seeks to understand the customer. By understanding the customer, a business is better able to create a marketing plan. After attracting the attention of a potential buyer, the business goal is for marketing to encourage a purchase.

A business writes a plan for how to manage the marketing activities of a product. This plan will include who the consumer will be, along with when the marketing will take place and how much it will cost. The plan will also include a hypothesis (educated guess) of the number of customers who will purchase the product. This plan is called a marketing plan. The marketing plan will organize the work of many people working together toward a company marketing goal.

A marketing goal provides a level to work toward for those working to sell a product. The goal may be a set number such as increasing the number of sales to 50,000 units. Or, the goal may be to increase customer satisfaction for the product, such as score a nine or higher on all survey results. A goal also helps marketing managers determine if the marketing efforts are successful by comparing actual results to the goal numbers.

A focused marketing plan will always work toward the **marketing goal.** Employees of the company (managers, salespeople, research teams) work with other businesses (magazines, TV stations, suppliers) to help a product meet a company goal.

1. One goal of marketing is to encourage a buyer to make a purchase. What can a company do to encourage a buyer to spend their money?

2. What words or pictures were used in a commercial or advertisement for a product that caught your attention?

STRATEGIZE

The Drawing Board

Newspaper Advertising

Imagine you are the owner of an ice cream shop.

Last Tuesday at 9:00 in the morning your ice cream delivery company arrived. At the same time your vendor arrived to re-fill your juice machine. The ice cream delivery worker wheeled in a cart of one flavor, then returned to his truck to get the next flavor. This was the pattern every Tuesday for the ice cream delivery, and your shop offers 28 flavors! The juice machine vendor began his delivery following the same path for the juice re-fills, one juice at a time.

Swish! Plop! Whoop! Plunk! The ice cream delivery person was bringing in the mango ice cream, and the juice company delivery person was bringing in the grape juice. One slipped, and the other tripped, and then both fell to the floor. The mango ice cream mixed with the grape soda and smelled yummy! You try a scoop - its amazing! You discovered a new flavor!

MANGO GRAPE

Create your ad in the space below for the local newspaper to tell of the new ice cream flavor.

CREATE

Why Study Marketing?

Marketing is vital to every company. Marketing brings customers to a business. Successful marketing gives customers the motivation to return time and again. As you explore different careers, you will notice that marketing has a part in every business. Working at a hotel, being a talent agent for an actor, fixing a computer, or managing a bank each use marketing to attract (and keep) customers wanting their products.

Did you know ... every item you touch has parts that were marketed and sold? Some everyday products, like cell phones, are made up of over 100 parts! Each of these parts were purchased by the manufacturing company, who then made the product. These businesses that purchased the parts are called manufacturers. A manufacturer will buy parts and then use them to create a finished product. The finished product is then ready to be sold to a customer.

What is a career you are considering? _____

What products will be sold by someone in this career?

_____

What do people who buy the products have in common?

_____

APPLY

Marketing Careers:

Ad Jingle Writer	Customer Service	Promotions Designer
Advertising Manager	Internet Ad Designer	Retail Sales Clerk
Brand Director	On-line Sales Agent	Social Media Agent
Celebrity Agent	Price Analyst	Sports Marketing Executive
Chief Marketing Officer	Product Photographer	Vice President of Marketing

Who Needs Marketing?

A baseball team signs a new pitcher and wants to tell the fans ... they need marketing.
A restaurant now offers pizza and wants to tell potential customers .. they need marketing.
A singing group releases a new song and wants to tell the fans ... they need marketing.
A hotel has a new location and wants to tell travelers ... they need marketing.
A toy company creates a fun shape pencil and wants to tell parents ... they need marketing.

Copyright Protected.

The Drawing Board

Show and Tell

Every good or service that is purchased uses a type of marketing to let potential customers know about the product. List any products that you choose below and include in the next box why that product needs marketing.

	Product	Why Does It Need Marketing?
1.	Hotel	To show travelers the beautiful hotel so they want to visit.
2.		
3.		
4.		
5.		
6.		
7.		

Consider the marketing careers listed on page 12. Select one career and fill in the space below answering the questions: Which career did you choose? What part do you think would be enjoyable? Why is this job needed in a company?

THINK

Product Marketing

New product marketing happens when a company is offering a product for the first time. The company is looking for new customers for the product. The marketing will help educate shoppers about the new item for sale.

The company creates a marketing plan to let consumers know:

- **Product Features**
- **The Product Price**
- **Where To Buy The Product**
- **Possible Sales & Discounts**

Did you know *new product marketing* is not only for recently invented products? A product may have been invented quite some time ago, but if it is the first time the company is selling the product, then a new product marketing plan will be created. The goal of the plan will be to tell customers the features and benefits of the new product. A new product marketing plan is needed for either a brand new invention or a product that the company is offering for the first time.

For example, face paint is a product in the marketplace offered by many sellers. CircusPals, Inc. is a company that has decided to start selling face paint in the company product line. Although face paint is not a completely new invention, at CircusPals selling face paint is a new idea.

CircusPals, Inc. has a second product they are ready to add to the product line. This second product is a brand new invention. The company has invented a blinking ink pen. The customer will write with the pen and then two minutes later the ink will begin to *blink* on and off. Never before seen! This is a new product at CircusPals, Inc. and also a new product to the marketplace.

For both of these examples the company will develop a new product marketing plan.

Product Line — All The Products Currently Being Sold By a Company.

Consider this:

An essential part of the success of the blinking ink pen will be the name of the product. A name should clearly tell the consumer what the product does as a feature. A product name should also be easy to remember.

Imagine you work at CircusPals. What would you suggest as two possible names for the ink pen invention?

_____

_____

THINK

The Drawing Board

Build The Plan

CircusPals, Inc. would like your help. The new face paint product is being developed and prepared for sale. The company is looking for new ideas to use in their marketing and advertising.

Fill in the blanks in each of the circles below to help the company develop the face paint product marketing plan.

- **Who Is The Target Customer That Will Buy The Product?** _____
- **Where would you market (advertise) the CircusPals face paint?** _____
- **What is one benefit to advertise of the product?** _____
- **Which retail store would sell a face paint product?** _____
- **What month of year will see the highest face paint sales?** _____
- **Similar face paint sells for $5 - $15. What price do you suggest?** $_____

Face Paint

CREATE

Searching For Success

A successful product can spend months, even years, in development. Even after all the time spent under development a product that is ready to be sold may not be successful. One reason a product fails to be successful may simply be due to a poor marketing plan decision. The customer will let a business know of a product failure by choosing not to purchase the product.

The product flaw may be due to many reasons including:

1. Poor Product Name
2. Price Too High
3. Poor Product Idea

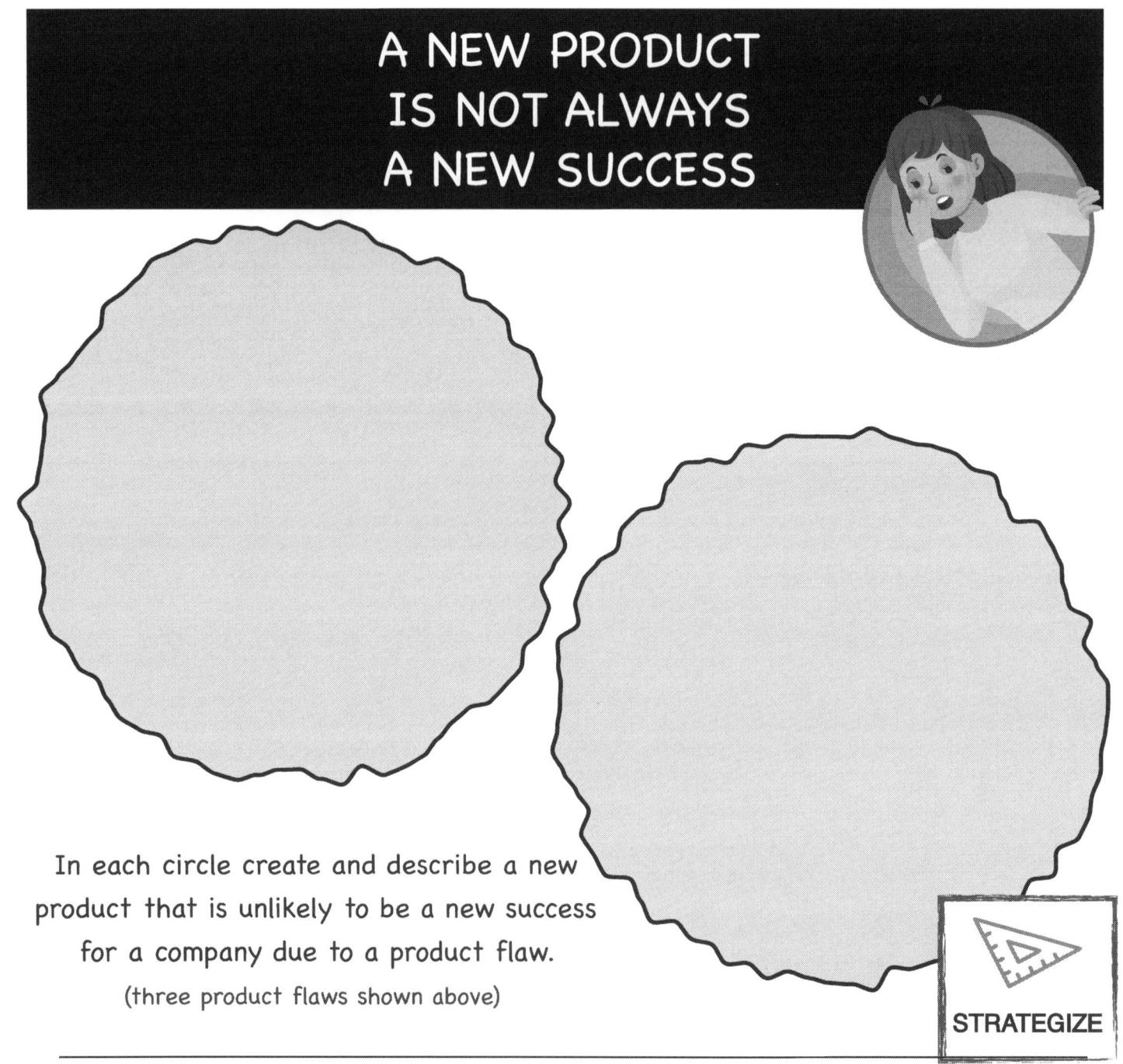

A NEW PRODUCT IS NOT ALWAYS A NEW SUCCESS

In each circle create and describe a new product that is unlikely to be a new success for a company due to a product flaw.

(three product flaws shown above)

STRATEGIZE

The Drawing Board

Make A Cash Cow

When a company is bringing a new product to market the hope is that the product will be an instant success. If marketing is successful and many customers buy the product it can be a cash cow for the company. "Cash Cow" is another way of saying a very successful product that earns the company a high profit.

Products benefit from the dedication and hard work of a team of people. Sometimes the marketing plan needs to be changed, or corrected, to help increase the chance of a products success.

Listed below is a product name, features of the product and the price of the product. In the last column circle which part of the marketing plan you believe was a problem, and therefore, a part of the reason the product did not succeed.

Product Name	Special Features	Price	Problem
1. Zip Color Crayons	Crayons where every line makes a rainbow of color.	$2.00	Poor Product Name / Price Too High / Poor Product Idea
2. Splash Water Light	Waterproof reading light for the bathtub.	$9.00	Poor Product Name / Price Too High / Poor Product Idea
3. Bark Bites	Organic dog food treats.	$24.00	Poor Product Name / Price Too High / Poor Product Idea
4. Sweat Sneakers	Sneakers with special stay-dry material that does not get wet.	$29.95	Poor Product Name / Price Too High / Poor Product Idea
5. Vitamin Chocolate	A chocolate bar with vitamins.	$14.95	Poor Product Name / Price Too High / Poor Product Idea

6. Select one of the products listed above in the chart. What would you suggest as a correction to the problem? What can the company do to improve the marketing?

_____
_____
_____
_____
_____

INVESTIGATE

Feature Marketing

A company celebrates when a product is successful. However, each product is successful only for a limited amount of time. Changes in technology and customer interests cause changes to the demand for a product. A product is successful as long as the sales of the product return a profit for the company.

> What is a profit?
> A company spends money to purchase a product to sell.
> Bills at a company include electric, payroll, advertising, rent, and more.
> A profit is the amount of money left after all the bills have been paid.
>
> **SALES - EXPENSES = PROFIT**

Company research continues after a product is introduced to the market. The research will study if customers still enjoy the product or if product updates are needed. Customers have needs and wants that change. What a customer was looking for when the product was purchased may be different a few months later. A company may add features, change materials, or update the advertising to tell more of what a shopper is looking to buy. Marketing updates to an already existing product may include a change in the package to add the words *new*, *improved*, or *updated*.

Example: DVD Movies

Before DVD movie players had been invented a customer could watch a movie at home using a VHS tape. Once the DVD player was invented customers began to want to purchase movies on a DVD disk, rather than a VHS tape. As the number of customers who wanted a DVD increased, a movie company had to change the marketing plan to meet customer demand for both VHS tapes and DVD's. DVD movies when first being sold were advertised as "Now Available On DVD". The number of consumers who wanted a DVD grew. Soon, all movies were available on both a VHS tape or a DVD. Customers expected the movie they wanted would be available on DVD. Over time more customers wanted DVD movies and fewer were seeking a VHS tape. As the shoppers preference changed from VHS to DVD a company would need to update the marketing plan. The updated marketing plan would tell the customer that the movie is now available in both a VHS and a DVD to satisfy the wants of the highest number of shoppers.

The Drawing Board

Product Updates

Royal Sports Company is a successful sports equipment company. The company manufactures and sells over 42 different sports balls. The company goal is to keep looking for new ways to improve the products. The company knows the product improvements will encourage buyers to stay loyal to the Royal Sports equipment brand. The Royal Sports customers seek the most up-to-date product on the market. To remain a customer favorite Royal Sports has a research team to develop new marketing ideas that help ensure a product is what a buyer wants or needs.

Royal Sports inventors just announced a new fabric for tennis balls. The new fabric on the tennis ball makes a ball glow at night. Another benefit of the new fabric is that the ball can hold in the air longer so it will bounce longer. The price will increase .89 cents a ball. Players can now play tennis at night. What are some sales bursts Royal Sports can add to the tennis ball package?

APPLY

Product Updates

When a customer has a change in what they want in a product, a company needs to update the product or risk losing the customer.

A company always wants to increase the number of customers. Getting more customers can be achieved with the help of marketing. Marketing can attract more customers to help a company sell more products.

When technology causes a change in what a customer wants, the company will need to update the product.

When a competitor changes a product in a way customers need, the company will need to update the product.

Technology → Twinkle Kids Toothpaste updated a kids toothpaste to be available in the colors blue and red. Glitter Toothpaste Company only offers toothpaste in green. The Glitter Toothpaste Company starts working to be able to offer customers blue and red color options.

Competition → "Did you try the new cheese french fries at Snack Hut?" As customers begin to talk about the delicious Snack Hut cheese fries a competitor, Lunch Shack, begins to research adding cheese french fries to their menu.

Buyer Habits → The Ivy Foundation has become a favorite charity among college students in Boston. The Ivy Foundation has chosen green shoelaces as a symbol of support. The buyer habits in Boston caused an increase in local green shoelace demand.

Government Laws → The government of each country passes laws or regulations during the year. Some of these new laws and regulations require a change to a component, or part, of a product.

The Drawing Board

Shopper Expectations

Eight Points A Customer Expects When Buying A Product

To Work As Advertised	Useful Features
Extended Warranty	Fair Price
Easy Return Process	Friendly Service
Helpful Instructions	Color and Size Options

A goal of marketing research
is to find new ideas to help a
company build a relationship between
the business and the customer.

Imagine You Are Shopping For A New TV.
Place in order the eight customer buying expectations shown at the bottom of the page.
1 would be the most important to you in a TV purchase, 8 would be the least important.

1. _____
2. _____
3. _____
4. _____
5. _____
6. _____
7. _____
8. _____

MOST IMPORTANT

LEAST IMPORTANT

EXPLORE

Copyright Protected.   www.YMBAgroup.com

Study The Competition

Direct Competition

Competition is when two or more businesses want to sell a product to the same group of customers. For example, does your town have more than one grocery store? The grocery stores compete with each other.

Direct competition means two or more businesses compete for the same customers. A business wants to be the first choice when a buyer goes shopping for a product. A business needs to be aware of the competitors products, the price of the products and exclusive discounts offered for their same or similar products.

Perhaps while shopping in the grocery store you noticed different brands of apple juice? Each of these apple juice brands compete with each other for a customer to choose their apple juice product. The apple juice brands are in direct competition.

Direct Competition   Indirect Competition

Indirect Competition

Indirect competition is important because it can take customers away from a business. When a potential customer can replace one product with another that meets the same need, the sellers of those products are indirect competitors.
For example:
Ice Peak Coat Company is a direct competitor with *Powder Ski Jackets, LLC*. Each company is very popular with shoppers who like to snowboard. A top seller each of the past three years has been warming socks that snowboarders wear over the standard sock. This helps keep the feet warm while in the snowboard boots.

    Recently *SV 2 Boot, Inc.* introduced a boot that has the warming sock integrated into the boot design. That is a benefit to the consumers who would have one less item to purchase and one less item to plan for when preparing to snowboard.

    Both businesses that sell the warming socks have an interest in the new product from SV 2 Boot, Inc. since it will replace the top-selling warming socks. Consumer demand will shift from wanting warming socks to selecting to purchase the boot that has the sock integrated into the boot design. SV 2 Boot is an indirect competitor with both Ice Peak Coat Company and Powder Ski Jackets.

The Drawing Board

Company Brands

How many different competitor brands can you list for each of the following products:

Sneakers: _____   _____   _____

Cereal: _____   _____   _____

Cars: _____   _____   _____

Toys: _____   _____   _____

Hotels _____   _____   _____

Gas Stations: _____   _____   _____

Direct Competitor
Grocery Store -> Grocery Store

Indirect Competitor
Car Rental Company -> Retail Car Store

Retail stores are direct competitors with other retail stores.

Inside retail stores you find brands that are direct competitors with other brands.

Look at the words below found on an updated products package. Circle which one is most likely to capture your attention.

Buy Me   I'm The Best   I Have A Low Price

I Have A Fancy Box   Earn Rewards!

STRATEGIZE

Copyright Protected.

The Four P's

Marketing includes all aspects of trying to sell a product. Marketing includes how the product is presented to a potential customer. To present the product in a consistent style, a marketing plan is used to organize all of the selling efforts. A marketing plan includes four main sections. These four sections are known as the *Four P's of Marketing*. By dividing the marketing efforts into these four categories each of the different departments working on the plan will be coordinated.

The four "P" categories are Product, Place, Promotion, and Price. Every marketing plan will develop a strategy that includes each of these four categories. When these four aspects are coordinated, a product has the highest chance of success.

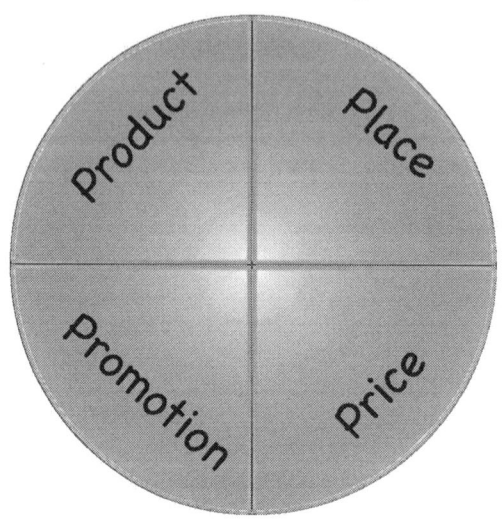

Product

The *product* in marketing may be either a good or a service. What is the difference between a good and a service? A good is tangible. Tangible means you can put your hands on it and touch it. A good is what you likely think of when you imagine walking into a store and buying something. A service is something someone does for you. You are not able to touch a service. You can not move a service and put it in a different location. A service business would include getting a hair cut, having a lawn mowed or visiting a doctor.

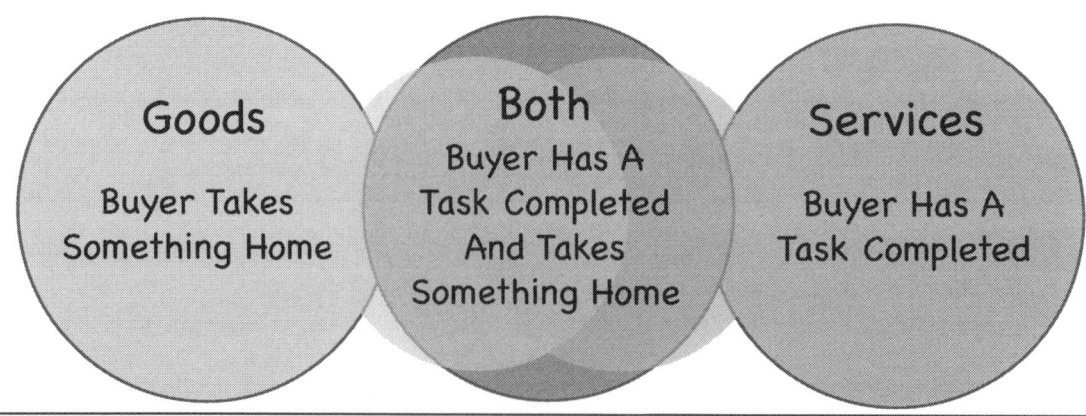

The Drawing Board

Good or Service?

Listed below are possible purchases that can be made by a customer. Write in the blank GOOD, SERVICE or BOTH to indicate what type of product is being purchased.

1. A volleyball net from an internet website. _____

2. Pizza served at a restaurant. _____

3. Annual teeth cleaning by a dentist. _____

4. Crayons from a catalog in the mail. _____

5. Printer ink for your home printer from the office supply store. _____

6. Pet food for your dog from the veterinarian at the exam. _____

7. Exercise weights from at a sports equipment store. _____

8. A custom imprinted award for your soccer coach. _____

9. A bounce house rental to be installed in the backyard Sunday. _____

10. Making a deposit into your savings account at your bank. _____

Marketing In Action

1. What is one good you saw someone purchase this past week?

2. What is one service you saw someone purchase this past week?

3. What is an example of a time when you or a family member purchased a good and a service at the same time?

THINK

Place

There are different ways a product arrives on the shelf at a retail store. The path of product to the consumer is called the *distribution channel*.

Sample Distribution Channels

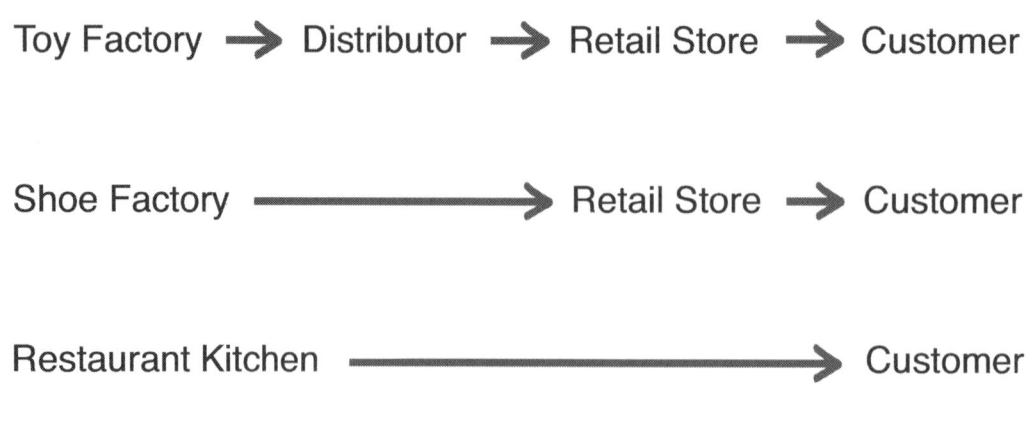

How the product gets to a customer is only one half of the "Place" category. The second part of the category is the actual location where the goods or services are purchased. There are many different locations in the marketplace where goods or services may be purchased. The marketing plan seeks to make each buying location part of an enjoyable purchase for the buyer. If a location is welcoming and helpful, the buyer will be more likely to purchase.

Marketplace Type	Marketplace Example
Door to Door Selling	Encyclopedia Sales Person
Factory Clearance Center	All-Mart Appliance Clearance
Internet Shopping	Website www.ShopHere.com
Mail Order Catalog	Pamela's Goodie Barn Catalog
Outlet Mall	Ace Shopping Outlet Mall
Professional Office	Doctors Office
Retail Store	Grocery Store
Television Station	SNB Network TV
Trade Show	Toy Industry Trade Show

The Drawing Board

Retail Floor Plan

Congratulations! You just became the manager at Twin Country. Twin Country is a clothing store focused on young adults 18-35 years old. In general, the customers who shop in the store buy 50% women's clothes, 25% accessories, 20% men's clothes and 5% children's clothes. Your regional manager has asked for your ideas on the store floor plan. Reminder, consider ideas that will make the store convenient for customers, so they want to stay and shop!

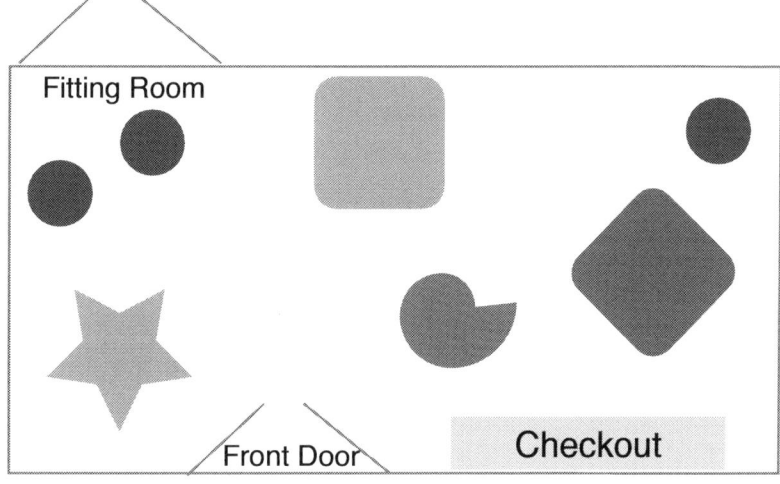

1. Why does the manager have the clearance discount racks in the back of the store?

2. The regional manager has placed the women's clothes section across the store from the fitting room and away from the baby and kid's section. What suggestions do you have on how this layout can be improved?

KEY

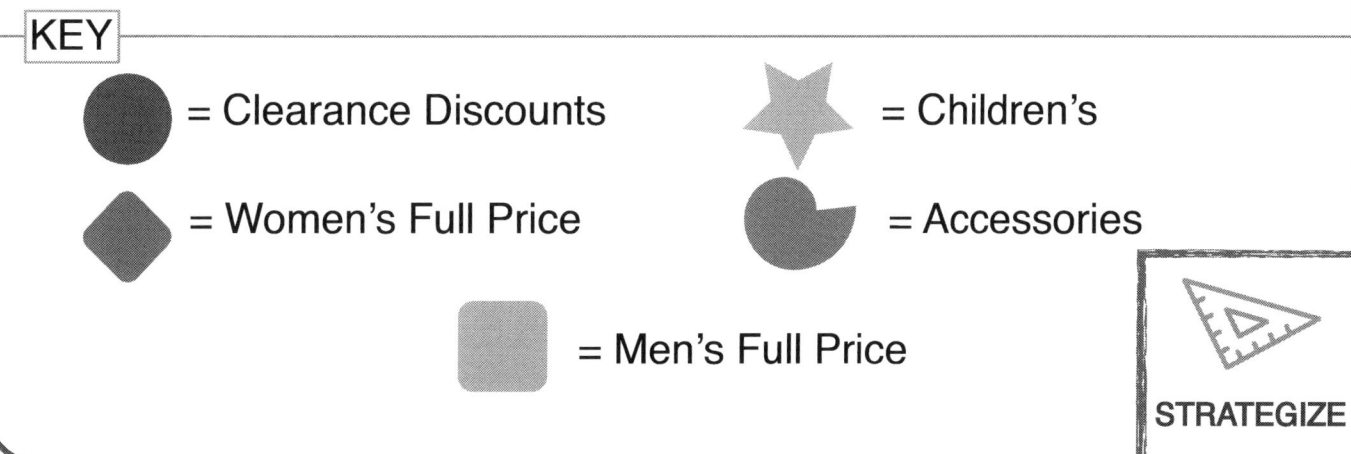

STRATEGIZE

Promotion

A company just decided to begin selling a new product. The manufacturing design is complete and the product is ready to sell. The stores receive the products, but how does a customer learn about the product? How will they know what the product offers? How will the need or want for the product be created? The answer to these questions is promotion. Promotion is the product advertising and special events that help customers learn about the product.

Promotion includes newspaper and magazine advertising, radio advertising, television commercials, coupons, team sponsorships, free samples, catalogs, postcard mailings, billboards, digital advertising (including website pop-up ads, social network postings), E-mail messages and more. In general, anywhere a company can show a company name, logo, or product is a form of marketing promotion.

Promotion also includes the product package. Generally packages are for products, not for services. While in a store a shopper can see shelves with package after package of items for sale. The packages can be thought of as small billboards or advertisements. Which box stands out on the shelf? Which box has an easy to read layout? Are the details, features, and benefits clear to see and easy to understand? The package may be the final chance a company has to convince a buyer to purchase.

The Drawing Board

Package Design

Look who just received a gift in the mail! Inside the wrapped box is an alarm clock. The alarm clock features are listed below. Design what you imagine the outside of the alarm clock box would have as a design. Use some or all of the details below in the design.

Be sure to include the company name and price on the box. What other details would be on the clock box to encourage buyers to purchase? How does the box design catch a buyers attention?

Alarm Clock Details

Brand Name: ClockTown USA, Inc.
Colors: Black, Blue, White
Price: $14.95
Power: Plug or Battery

Feature: Large, Easy Read Numbers
Feature: Two Different Alarm Sounds
Feature: $3 Coupon Off Batteries Inside
Feature: Small Design, Easy For Travel

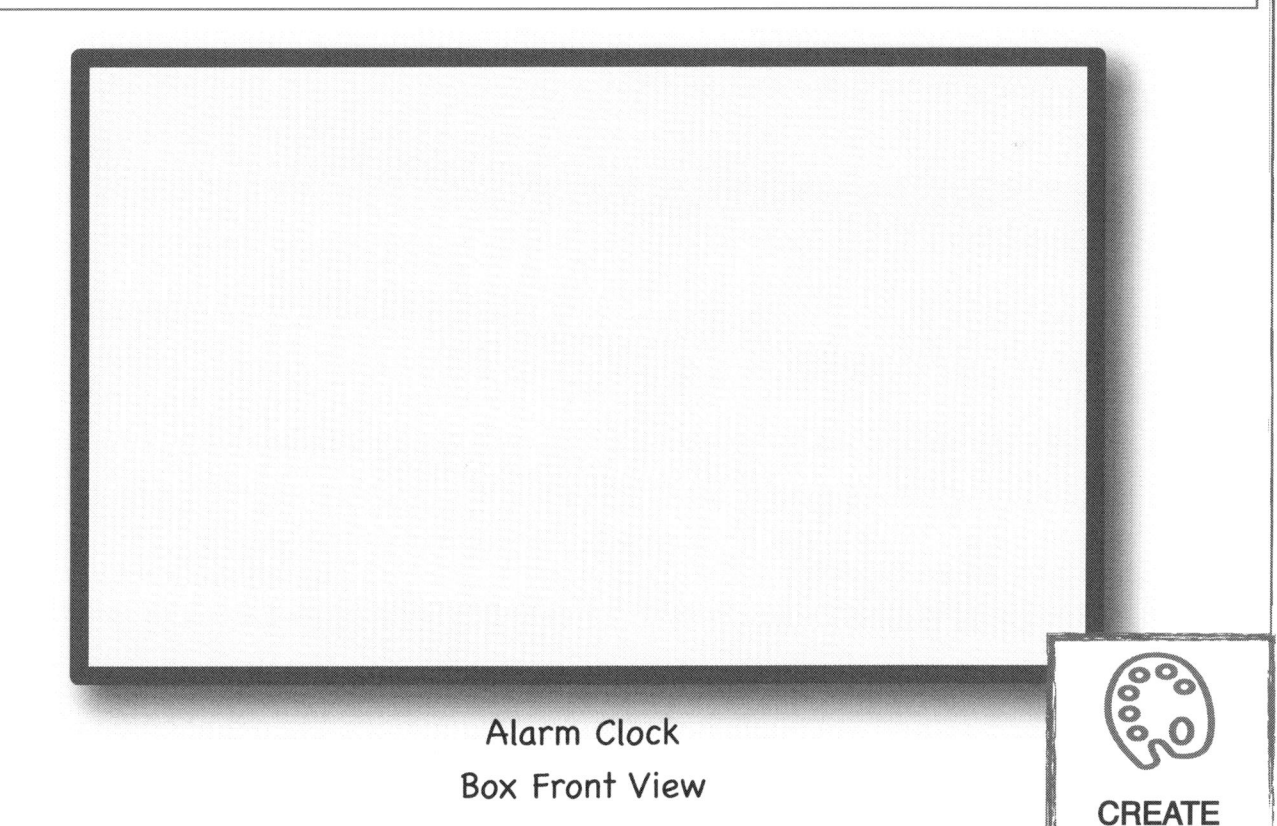

Alarm Clock
Box Front View

CREATE

Price

The last "P" in the four P's of marketing is "Price". A correct price can attract customers, but a price too high may prevent a customer from making a purchase. The price of the product is one of the most important product decisions. For a customer to have an interest in purchasing a product based on price there are three points to consider:

(1) The price has to be in a range a customer can afford to pay.
(2) The customer must feel the product is a good value for the cost.
(3) Competitor products should be priced approximately the same.

Price out of range .... A fancy sports car by Koni Motors Company with many modern digital upgrades may catch a potential car buyer's attention, but what is the price? In this case, the price of $85,000 would result in many interested buyers not being able to purchase the car.

Competitor price much lower ... Neptune Motors, Inc. is offering a family car for $24,000. Steel Auto Company, the competition, has a similar family car at a price of $19,995. The advertising for Neptune Motors will need to include an explanation to potential buyers to explain how the Neptune Motors car is a good value and worth the higher cost. If the Neptune marketing does not show potential buyers the added benefits many shoppers will view, the Steel Auto Company car as being a better value. Buyers will then purchase the Steel Auto Company car.

When a price is decided for a product both numerical data and emotional data should be considered. In many cases shoppers feel that numbers ending in a 5 or 9 are less expensive than prices that end in other numbers. The perception is that $49.99 is a much better value than $50.00 even though the savings is only one penny. Once a price is set for a product, a business may later choose to make price changes. The price of a product is researched and updated to hopefully return a profit to the company that is selling the product.

Numerical Price Data	Emotional Price Data
What is the cost to produce?	Is the price ending in a 5 or 9?
What is the cost to market?	Is this a want or a need?
What are the competitor prices?	Does the brand have added value?
What is the overhead cost*?	Any special incentives to buy?

*Overhead cost is the cost to run the business such as taxes, electric, payroll. This does not include the direct costs to make the product, such as product parts and package materials.

The Drawing Board

A Nice Price

Below is a list of everyday products. Imagine that you are the price manager at The Rapid Shop Company. Your task today is to set a price for each of these items. The goal of the price is for it to be one that the customer will find most appealing. At a fast, quick, first glance – which price is most appealing?

Hint: The most eye-catching price is not always the lowest price.

	Product	Most Eye-Catching Consumer Price		
1.	1 bag of potato chips	80¢	74¢	75¢
2.	1 medium pizza	$4.95	$4.80	$4.97
3.	2 baseballs	99¢	$1.00	90¢
4.	2 ice cream cones	98¢	88¢	95¢
5.	10 pencils	49¢	47¢	50¢
6.	4 notebooks	$4.95	$4.92	$4.97
7.	3 cookies	99¢	96¢	98¢
8.	1 jump rope	80¢	72¢	75¢
9.	6 strawberries	86¢	89¢	90¢
10.	8 balloons	$5.55	$5.56	$5.53

11. How many prices above did you circle that end with the numbers 5 or 9? _____

12. Review the prices you circled above. How many did you choose that were the actual lowest price on the line? _____

13. Why do you think someone would not always circle the lowest price?

_____

_____

APPLY

Copyright Protected.

The Company Image

What is PUBLIC RELATIONS?

Promotion includes public relations. Public relations is a marketing term abbreviated as "PR" that is used to describe the management of a potential customers impression of the company. Public relations is often not specifically about a single product, but rather about the company overall. *Does the company treat the customers well? Are earth-friendly chemicals used? Will the company lend assistance when people need help? Is the company interested in assisting the community?*

What is a BRAND?

The name of a company or product, usually placed with a logo, create a brand. A brand is recognized by customers and is often known to belong to a specific company. Some industries heavily market around a brand. For example, a sneaker company has the brand logo on the sneaker. The shopper wants to wear the brand and this has an added value. The added value is from feeling pride or belonging to a group when wearing the brand.

The Drawing Board

Public Impressions

Public Relations

A company has an image in the marketplace. The image is how potential customers view the company. Company loyalty is when a customer is dedicated to a specific brand or company. This loyalty may be based on national charity events or local community assistance by the company.

1. What are some ways a company can offer help in a community?

2. What can a company do to keep current customers happy?

3. How could a business lend a hand when urgent help is needed?

4. What marketing can a business use to keep the company name in the mind of potential customers in a community?

The Brand Logo

A brand logo is a picture or design that customers identify with a specific company. Look around the room and identify a company logo or brand name. Make a list in the blanks below. Find ten and you are a logo superstar!

1.   6.

2.   7.

3.   8.

4.   9.

5.   10.

INVESTIGATE

Marketplace Selling

The marketplace is where the buyer and seller meet, and products are purchased. The marketplace can be a retail store where customers walk inside and the products are ready for purchase. A marketplace may also be in-person or on an internet website. When a purchase is made on-line at a website the customer was able to view the product from a computer. A customer may also purchase a product by calling a company and requesting to place an order on the phone.

The key to being successful in a marketplace is for a company to make the purchase process easy and enjoyable for the customer. Most retail stores have set times the store will open and close. The time to close is helpful to allow the store to clean and re-stock items. The internet marketplace is a unique opportunity for a company. The on-line internet marketplace is open 24 hours a day, seven days a week. By having a website where buyers may shop, a company can increase the total number of products sold since the longer store hours better accommodate, or workaround, a shoppers schedule.

When preparing a marketplace, one consideration is who will be the customer shopping at the location. In marketing, understanding the customer is called knowing your customer demographics. Customer demographics may be based on age, where they live (geography), if there are any children in the home (family size), hobbies, urgency, and the amount of time the buyer has to purchase and more.

※ ※ ※ ※ ※

> The demographics of the customer will help the company better meet the needs and wants of the shoppers. By understanding the different groups in the marketplace and studying each segment the marketing can better satisfy customer wants and needs. When RoadCare, Inc. was placing an ad in the local newspaper they considered what a large number of the customers had in common. The company conducted research and found most customers purchased a RoadCare package to provide help when they had a flat tire and were stranded on the side of the road. As a result of the research RoadCare used the line in the advertisement, *We Are There In A Flash*. For the customer receiving help promptly was crucial. An advertisement line such as, "Our Drivers Take Their Time" would not meet the rapid response wants of the customer.

The Drawing Board

Needs and Wants

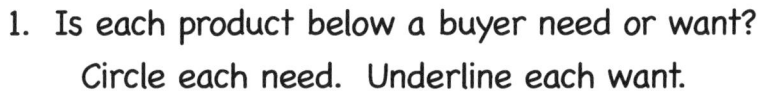

1. Is each product below a buyer need or want?
   Circle each need. Underline each want.

Water
Puppy Dog
Bottled Water
Medicine
Scented Shampoo
Notebook With A Sparkle Cover
Designer Medicine Case
Bar of Soap
Video Game
A Place To Live

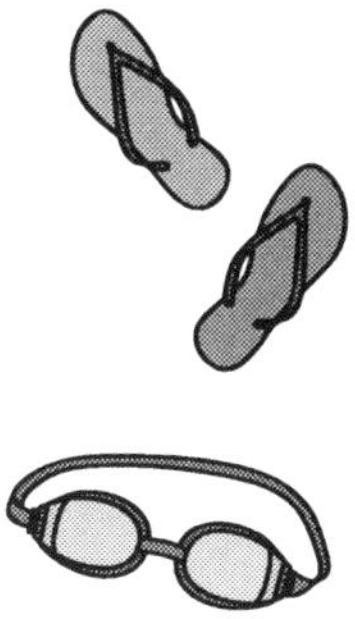

When A "Need" Becomes A "Want"

Did you know a company can convince a customer that a "want" is a "need"?

2. Imagine you are shopping for hand soap. Generally you purchase the store brand at $1.49 for two bars of soap. While in the store, you see a display in the isle that catches your attention. The soap company, Sudzy, is offering three bars of new lemon luxury scented soap for $2.79. What would some buyers do, and why?

_____

_____

Determine if the buyer situation below is an **urgent need to buy** or **time to shop**.

3. You start a new job tomorrow and need a suit. _____

4. It is 8:00 p.m. you need to feed your dog and are out of dog food. _____

5. Next month you are taking a vacation and need a bathing suit. _____

6. Thanksgiving decorations just began to be placed out in stores. You need shoes for New Years Eve. _____

EXPLORE

AIDA Is Here To Help

A company has a daily goal of selling products and services. AIDA is an abbreviation to summarize the steps to take when creating a promotional plan. AIDA has four stages. Step one is to attract the **attention** of the potential customer. The second step is to hold the **interest** of the potential customer. Step three is to build a **desire** (want) in the customer for the product or service. Step four is to encourage the buyer to take **action** and purchase the product.

After a company sells a product or service, the new goal becomes to build a loyal customer relationship. A company may offer membership clubs and coupons to encourage buyers to return for future purchases. This pattern is repeated again and again for each shopper who is considering a purchase.

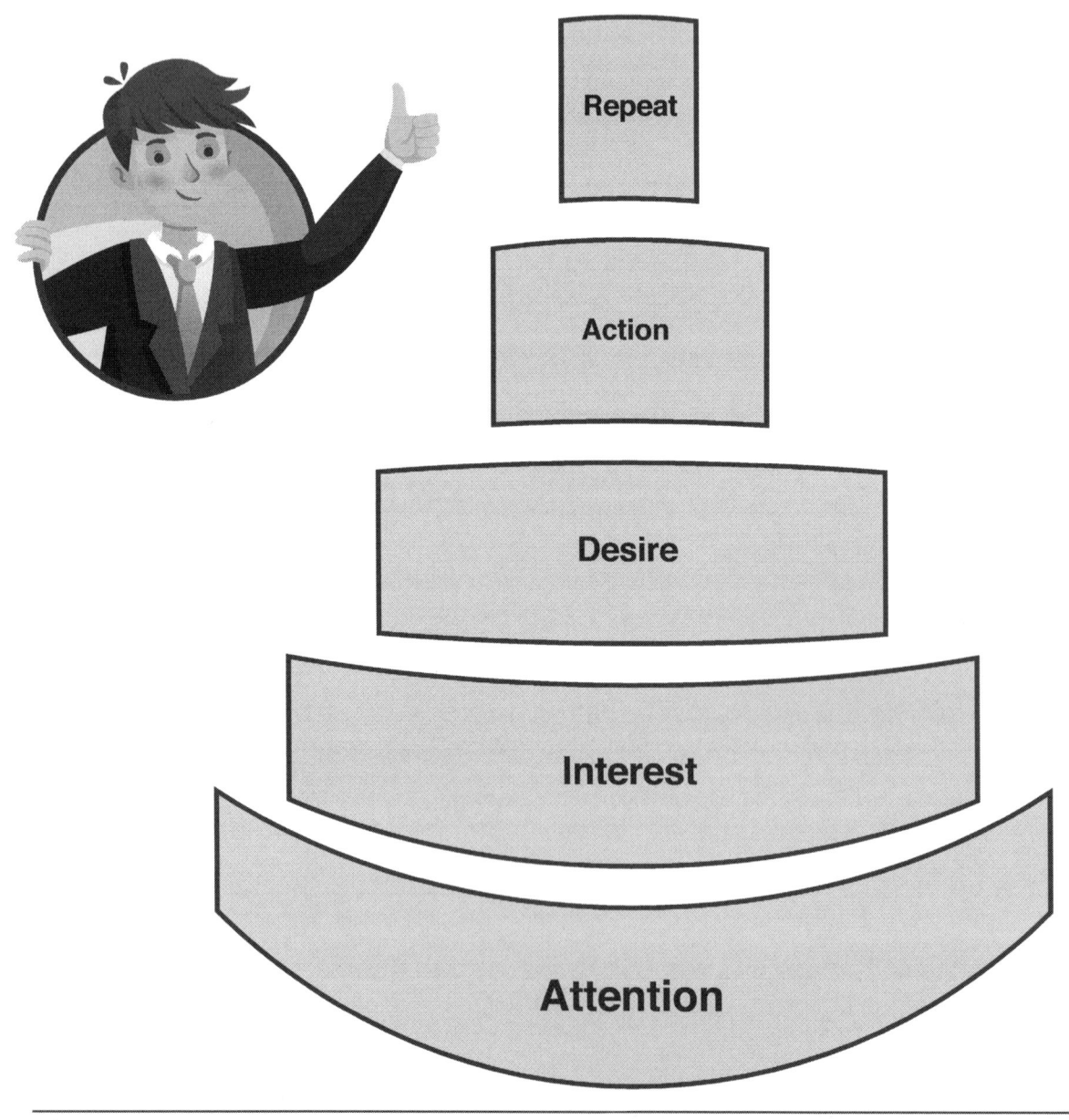

The Drawing Board

Attention Shoppers

A.I.D.A.

2 Interest

1 Attention

3 Desire

4 Action

Win A Free Guitar!

New! Junior Guitar

1 DAY

One Day Only!

Enter To Win A Junior Guitar
This Saturday, August 29th
9:00 am - 7:00 pm

Modern Guitar Design
20% Off Any Guitar Case

See You There!

All 4 Music Stop 142 Main Street
Cleveland, Ohio

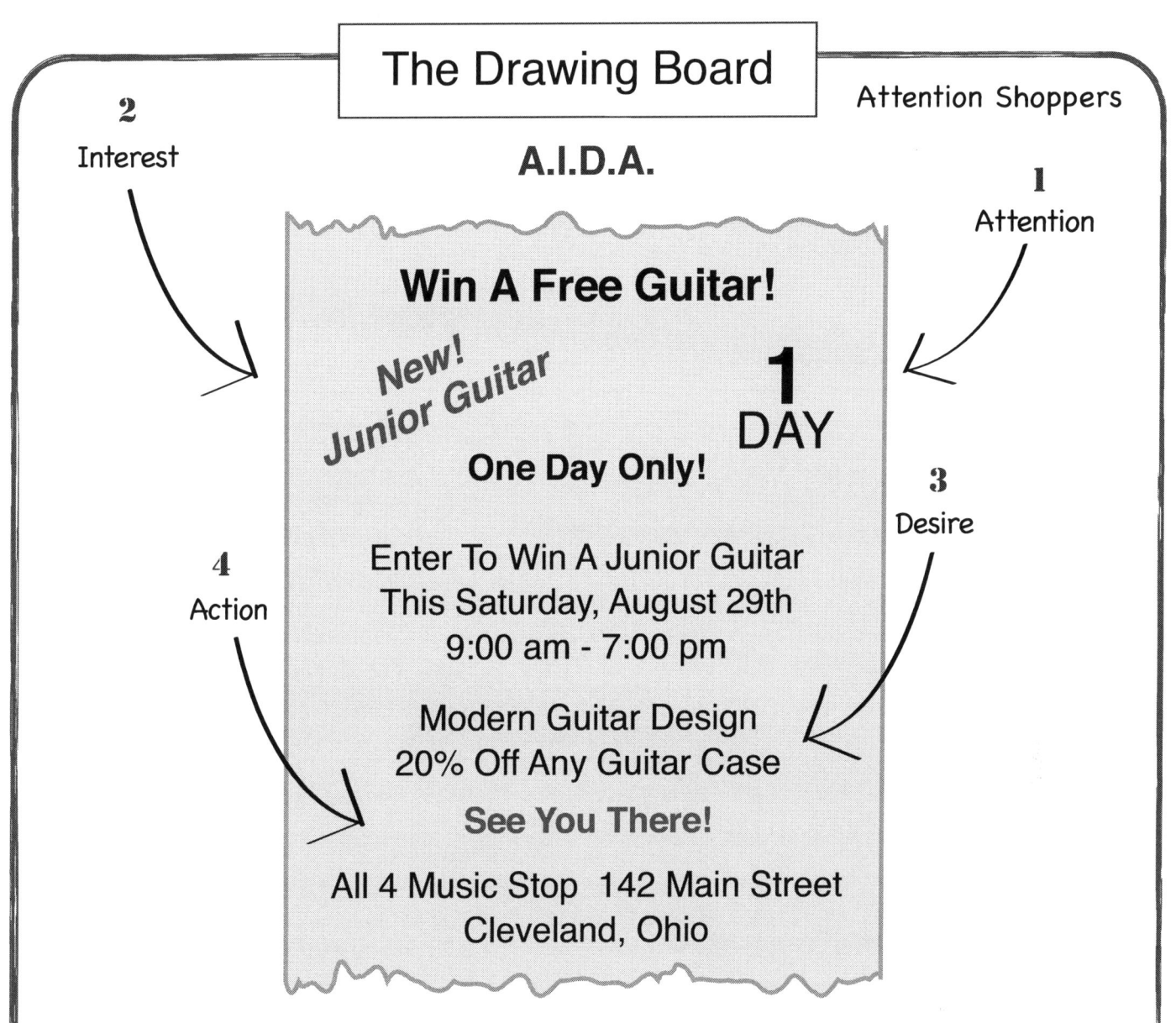

Imagine you are the manager at Cookies Chip Shop. A new cookie named the Pizza Cookie is being first offered for sale on October 1 at the local County Fair.

1. What would you write in the advertisement to catch a customers "Attention"?

2. What would you write to keep the "Interest" of a buyer?

3. What would you write to increase the "Desire" in a buyer for the product?

4. What would you write to encourage a buyer to take "Action"?

APPLY

Follow The Data

The marketing plan seeks to meet the needs and wants of potential customers. To gain the attention of a potential customer, a company gathers feedback from buyers in the marketplace. The feedback is examined with sales results to understand the needs and wants of customer's. The marketing plan will then be adjusted to try to keep the product in the "moving" and "maximum" growth stages of the product life-cycle.

What is a product life-cycle?

A product moves from one stage in the market to the next stage in a generally predictable order. These stages in the market are called the life-cycle of a product. Different customers decide to purchase at different times in the life-cycle. Knowing the stage in the life-cycle will help a marketing message be created with current customers needs and wants in mind. For example, a buyer who waits two years to buy new technology is possibly looking for a good deal and clear directions inside the package.

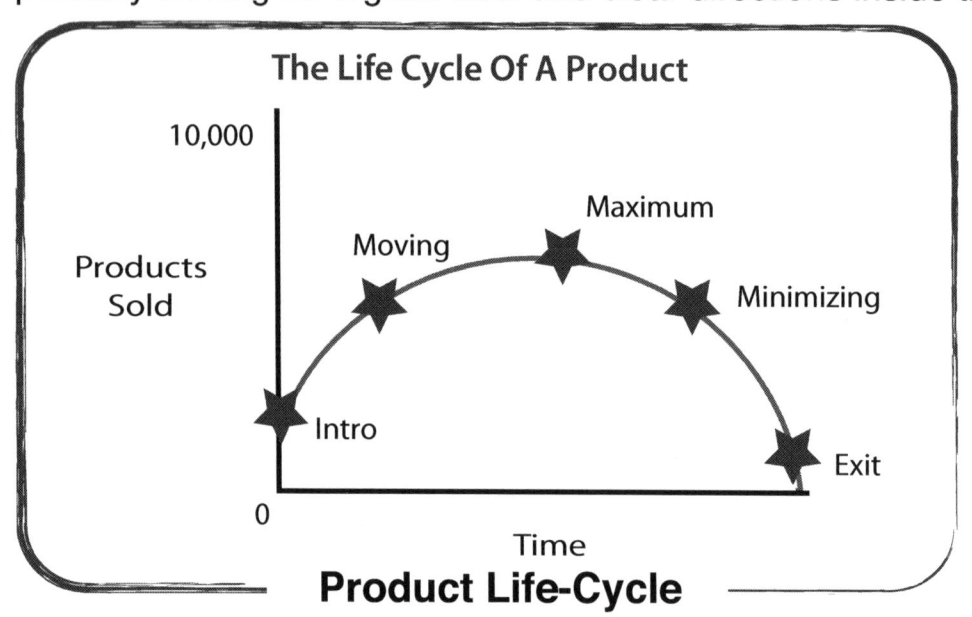

The Life Cycle Of A Product

(Graph: Products Sold (0 to 10,000) vs Time, showing stages: Intro, Moving, Maximum, Minimizing, Exit)

Product Life-Cycle

Intro - The introduction of a product to the marketplace.

Moving - The product is successful and customers continue to purchase.

Maximum - The peak of product success. The highest number of products are sold.

Minimizing - The number of purchases made decreases. The sales are lower possibly due to a new technology or a competitor product at a lower price.

Exit - The product does not have enough sales to make a profit for the company. The product will no longer be manufactured or offered for sale.

The Drawing Board

Product Decisions

A marketing plan needs to be aware of the current life cycle stage of a product. This will help a company make marketing decisions that better meet potential customer needs and wants. Responding to needs and wants in a marketing message will help a company attract buyers.

1. What are two promotion ideas that may be used when introducing a new product?
_____

2. Why do you think products are not able to always be in the "moving" stage?
_____

3. At the "maximum" stage the product has the most customer demand. When there is a lot of customer demand the product price will increase. At the "maximum" stage is it likely or unlikely coupons will be offered for the product? Why?
_____

4. During the "minimizing" stage demand from customer's for the product goes down. Since there is less demand for the product what do you think will happen to the price?
_____

5. A change in technology may be a reason for a product to enter the "exit" stage of the life cycle. What is one product that was no longer demanded (needed) by the customer due to a change in technology? _____
_____

6. Two years ago 10,000 happy shirts were sold. Last year 7,000 happy shirts were sold. This year it is expected that 4,000 happy shirts will be sold. What stage of the product life cycle does this describe? _____

7. Hot-Z Fitness Gym opened last year. The gym already has 85 more members than the competitor. What stage of the product life cycle does this describe? _____

8. Flight Weight Company just spent $18,000 on radio advertisements in the Northeast to tell customers about their new product, travel size exercise weights. What stage of the product life cycle does this describe?
_____

EXPLORE

Research Questions

Research gives a company knowledge about how people in the market view the product the company is trying to sell. By understanding what a customer may need or want the marketing plan can be more effective. There are different types of questions a company can use to gather details about potential customers, their opinions and changes in buying trends.

What Is A Trend? A trend is a pattern that is revealed when looking at the research results. A trend may be something that happens over a long time, such as decades, or a short time, such as hours. Researching a trend will help a company make decisions that better meet buyer needs and wants.

Leading and Non-Leading Questions

A successful research survey will ask Non-Leading Questions. Leading questions will include an opinion in the question. "Educated people prefer orange juice more than grape juice, don't you?" is a leading question. Non-leading questions present only the question without encouraging one answer over another. A non-leading question is, "Which do you prefer, orange juice or grape juice?"

Closed and Open-Ended Questions

A successful research survey will ask Open Ended Questions. A closed question is one that only requests a yes or no answer. Closed questions do not gather a lot of information. "Do you like blue shirts?" The yes or no answer does not provide the company with useful information. Open-ended questions invite a response that goes beyond the yes or no with details about why a customer has a feeling or opinion.

What is a focus group?

A company may gather research about potential customers on a written survey, an internet survey or a Focus Group. A focus group is usually about 5 to 15 people who are asked questions in person by an interviewer. The interviewer will gather the answers and observe the interactions among the people as they answer. For example, if one member of the focus group says, "The new dressing rooms are too small" and the majority of focus group members nod their heads and agree. The data and the observations will tell the company that their dressing room size is a problem to correct.

The Drawing Board

The Correct Question

Leading Questions and Non-Leading Questions

Non-leading questions are important to gathering useful marketing research. Below are four survey questions. Circle each question to show if it is leading or non-leading.

1. Everyone adores the new sandwich shop in town. Do you think they like it?

   Leading   Non-Leading

2. Rate how much you enjoy the tomato soup. 1 for not much, 10 for very much.

   Leading   Non-Leading

3. Up to 10, how many stars would you give the waitress at your table today?

   Leading   Non-Leading

4. How do you think the restaurant is kept so clean?

   Leading   Non-Leading

Open Ended Questions and Closed Questions

Open-ended questions encourage a detailed answer. Closed questions only seek a one-word answer. There are not many details learned from closed-ended questions. When a company is trying to understand potential customers more detailed replies are more helpful. Open ended questions give more information to market researchers.

5. Did you try the new fresh-baked bread?

   Open Ended   Closed

6. How could we have better served you today?

   Open Ended   Closed

7. In your opinion, was your lemonade cold?

   Open Ended   Closed

8. Why did you choose to visit here today?

   Open Ended   Closed

APPLY

Goods and Services

A company is in business to sell products. The product may be either a *good* or a *service*. Marketing for either a good or a service will use the 4 P's of Marketing. The 4 P's are product, place, promotion, and price.

There are different ways to sell when marketing a service rather than a good to a customer. Below are two storefront marketing posters. The first is for Puzzle Palace, Inc., and the second is for Quick Chops Hair Cut Company.

GOOD

Holiday Gifts!
Come Back To See
Our New Puzzles.
Bring A Friend
Save 10%

Puzzle Palace
Retail Store Selling Goods

SERVICE

Stop In Today
Always Here
Quick Hair Cuts
Little Time,
Big Style.

Quick Chops Hair Cuts
Retail Store Selling Services

Marketing for a good will focus on service, but is likely also to include a discount to help the customer know about a new or updated good that is available.

Marketing for a service often will tell a customer the service is available anytime. Service marketing has a focus on time, convenience, quality, and satisfaction.

Puzzle Palace is running a marketing campaign that seeks to find new customers and to encourage past customers to return to shop again. By offering a discount as an incentive to a customer the company goal is to motivate people to talk about the store. Marketing for a good often includes an advertising suggestion for a buyer to visit the store and see the product in person.

Quick Chops Hair Cuts is offering a service. Therefore the marketing campaign has a slightly different goal than Puzzle Palace. At Quick Chops Hair Cuts customers are encouraged to return again and again. The company knows hair grows and that the people who live in the area will need to have a haircut. By including the words "Always Here" on the window advertisement, customers are encouraged to remember the company is available. Quick Chops is also seeking new customers and points out the fast service and big style to capture the attention of a buyer.

The Drawing Board

Identify The Service

A company uses marketing to sell a product. A product may be either a good, a service, or both a good and a service. Shown below are business names. Indicate if the product the business will sell is likely to be a good, a service or both. In the last column, write what you think could be one product sold by the company.

Company Name	Good, Service, or Both	Product Sold
1. Music Mania Co.		
2. The Icing Shop		
3. United Gas Station		
4. Pizzaz Magic Shop		
5. Sparkle Nail Spa Co.		
6. Regal Bank, LLC		
7. Boating Fun Company		
8. Reds Auto Repair Co.		

THINK

Service Marketing

> How is marketing different when the product being sold is a service rather than a good?

Marketing is used by a company to attract customers to buy a product. When selling a good that the customer can see, feel, and take home, the marketing shows attractive pictures of the item. The customer then wants the product and may make a purchase. But when selling a service, what pictures can be used in the advertisement?

Service buyers are shopping for a task they want to have completed. At times the task is one the buyers do not know how to do (a new roof). A service buyer may also shop for a task they do not want to do (tax forms). In both cases, the buyer is looking for a company that has the reputation of being skilled and reliable. Therefore, a primary goal of service advertising is for the advertising to include images of professional employees and satisfied customers.

Service advertising will often show professional employees helping a customer in need. The need of the customer in the advertisement can be due to three different events:

(1) **Envy** - happens when the possible customer is watching someone in the advertisement which used the company service. Seeing the advertisement makes the potential customer want the service. An example of this would be a commercial that shows a car with a flat tire. The company selling the product arrives quickly to change the tire. The message being told in the commercial is that being a customer of the company selling the service makes your life better.

(2) **Fear** - is shown when the customer in the advertisement is in a scary situation and needs the assistance of the company selling the service. An example of this would be a radio commercial telling the listener a tornado is about to arrive at a small town. A family may be shown trying to gather their favorite belongings and wondering what they will do. The commercial ends by saying, "Snuggle Blanket Insurance, You Are Not Alone."

(3) **Ability** - has a customer in the advertisement that is not able to complete a task and wishes they had made arrangements for the company selling the service to help. An example would be a homeowner at the top of a tall ladder trying to clean gutters on their home. The ladder looks wobbly; the job seems dangerous. The advertising message is that contacting the company selling the service is a relaxing and safe choice.

The Drawing Board

Sell The Service

bank teller	waitress	landscaper	insurance agent
sports coach	carpet installer	fitness trainer	hairstylist

Select a service industry job shown in the box above. Next, design a newspaper advertisement below for the local paper. The goal of the advertisement is to get the attention of new potential customers. Before you begin, first consider who your target customer will be and what your company is looking to sell.

Be sure to include the 4 P's of marketing in the advertisement.

Product, Place, Promotion, and Price

Who is the target potential customer that you hope will visit your location after seeing the advertisement?

CREATE

Service The Customer

An employee represents the company. In many cases, an employee communicating with a customer is the last chance a company has to convince a shopper to make a purchase. An employee may also be the reason a shopper chooses to not make a purchase. For this reason having effective customer service skills is important in every industry.

To excel at customer service, an employee should:
- ✓ Satisify the basic needs of each customer at every interaction.
- ✓ Look for a moment in each interaction to go beyond what a customer expects.
- ✓ Greet every customer with a smile and with full effort and energy.

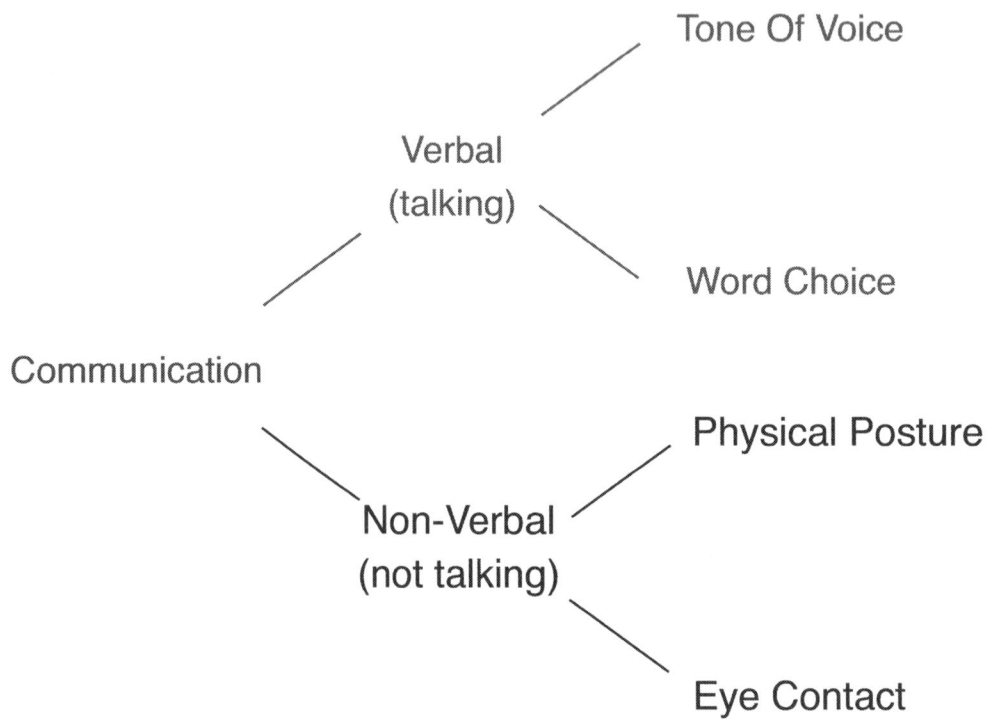

Communication
- Verbal (talking)
  - Tone Of Voice
  - Word Choice
- Non-Verbal (not talking)
  - Physical Posture
  - Eye Contact

Service Feedback

Feedback helps a company determine if they are meeting the expectations of shoppers. Feedback also provides a way to understand if employees are adequately trained. A customer is more likely to comment when they are unhappy rather than satisfied. A business will receive feedback more often when a shopper is disappointed, rather than when they are satisified.

Idea: Let an employee at a company know a time when you were a customer and appreciated the effort they made to provide excellent service. Write a letter to the store manager to share the details about your positive experience with an employee. Be sure to include how the experience made your shopping day more enjoyable.

The Drawing Board

Decision Scenarios

Listed below are four marketing questions to consider. Using full sentences write your answers below.

1. Bon Yummie Incorporated is your favorite restaurant. To appreciate you as a return customer the head chef notices your reservation and prepares a special meal. The food you are paying for is a good. But the restaurant also provides services. What are some services provided by the restaurant?

2. Imagine you are at TV-Pa-Looza, Inc. where you work as the repair manager. Last month the store repaired 42 televisions. Next month the store expects twice as many customers. How many televisions should you expect to repair?

3. Chilly 'N Cold, LLC is a service company, but when a customer needs a part of the air conditioner replaced the company will also sell the replacement item. Although the company sells parts for products, it is known as a service company. Why is Chilly 'N Cold called a service company and not a goods company?

4. Tropical Tours, Inc. is a resort hotel. The hotel offers a shark experience tour for the guests. Why would it be necessary for Tropical Tours to have excellent customer service when selling the shark experience tour?

STRATEGIZE

Wholesale Customers

A manufacturer is a company that makes goods in a factory.

These goods are later going to be sold to the customer in a retail store.

How do the products get to the retail store from the factory?

Products move from the factory to a retail store with the help of a wholesaler. The wholesale company is the customer of the manufacturer. The wholesale company will arrange for goods from the factory to be available and delivered to retail stores. The wholesale company is in the middle between the manufacturer who makes the products and the retail location that sells the products.

MADE
- Manufacturer — A product is made in a factory.

ORDERED
- Wholesaler — Products are ordered from the factory.

DELIVERED
- Retail Store — Products are delivered to the retail store.

BOUGHT
- Customer — A customer buys the goods in a retail store.

A wholesale business is beneficial to a manufacturer. The wholesaler will contact and negotiate prices and delivery with the retail store. Wholesalers allow the manufacturing company to focus on the production of the products. With each person in the process of bringing a product from production to the retail store each task is more efficient. A manufacturing company becomes a specialist in making goods. A wholesaler becomes a specialist in how to move the goods. A retail store becomes a specialist in how to meet the needs of the customers. Together they each share the common goal of selling products to customers.

The Drawing Board

Search and Solve

CUSTOMER	PLACE	PROMOTION	SALE
GOOD	PRICE	RESEARCH	SERVICE
MARKET	PRODUCT	RETAIL	STORE

Complete the word search below. Find all the words from the word box above.

```
N  G  O  O  D  J  I  Z  V  E
P  R  O  M  O  T  I  O  N  V
K  P  L  A  C  E  I  A  R  P
M  A  R  K  E  T  P  E  E  R
P  R  I  C  E  R  M  C  S  E
F  U  V  B  O  O  S  I  E  T
F  V  Z  D  T  T  E  V  A  A
L  K  U  S  O  L  B  R  R  I
E  C  U  R  A  A  U  E  C  L
T  C  E  S  P  H  Z  S  H  R
```

Unscramble the following words. Use the word box at the top of the page for ideas.

1. TIELRA _____

2. REMKAT _____

3. ALPCE   _____

4. CIPRE   _____

5. ELSA   _____

INVESTIGATE

Target Markets

Have you noticed the many products for hobbies and interests when looking for a way to spend time? With so many choices how does a company stand out? What can a business do to increase the chances of catching a potential buyer's attention in a busy marketplace? To increase the possibility of a buyer seeing a specific product, businesses use research to identify the target market.

The target market includes people with similar traits who the company thinks will enjoy a product. These specific traits will be used in advertising, packaging, and promotions to show the potential buyer how the product is a match to their lifestyle. The features to include in the product advertising are potential customers needs, wants, likes, and opinions. Including these details will increase the chance that the target market will notice the marketing.

For example, Queno Car Company is marketing for their new car. The car is small, very fuel efficient, and easy to park in tight spaces. The trendy car fits the lifestyle of people who live in the city and park in crowded areas. Queno is known for cars that are expensive due to their extra features such as a sunroof and DVD player. The target market is stylish adults with a high salary who reside in a crowded town or city.

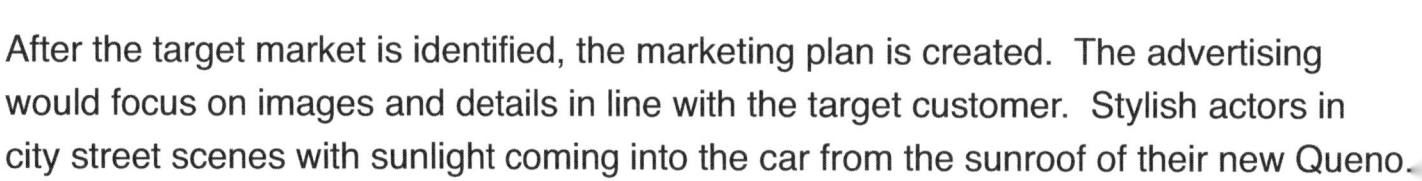

After the target market is identified, the marketing plan is created. The advertising would focus on images and details in line with the target customer. Stylish actors in city street scenes with sunlight coming into the car from the sunroof of their new Queno.

When a company completes the research and decides who the target market will be for a specific product, they can begin to design a promotion. For example, after Queno Car Company determined the target market for the new car they began to look for an event that the company could sponsor to promote the car. The annual food festival "Big City Organic Eats" became a natural choice. The company decided to give a car away at the event. By giving away a car at this event many potential customers in the target market will see and learn about the new product.

The Drawing Board

Pick A Market

Identify the target market. Draw a line from the product in the left column to the likely target market in the right column. Remember, a target market is the group of buyers being advertised toward that is most likely to purchase a product.

Product	Target Market
Two-2-Go Baby Stroller	Target Market: Age 20-40 Location: National Interest: New Parents
Fitness Restore Health Water	Target Market: Age 20-40, Female Location: National Interest: Team Sports
Fresh Sports Flower Scented Bags	Target Market: Age 20-40 Location: National Interest: Fitness
Pet360 Handy Vacuum	Target Market: Age 40-60 Location: National Interest: Crafts
Ciz-Or Fabric Cutters	Target Market: Age 20-40 and 40-60 Location: North USA Interest: Winter Sports
365 Solar Sun Glasses	Target Market: Age 20-40 and 40-60 Location: National Interest: Animals
Rugged Turf Snow Boots	Target Market: Age 15-20 and 20-40 Location: South USA Interest: Outdoors

APPLY

Create A Commercial

A television commercial can reach a large number of possible customers, however, it is a costly marketing option for a company.

The advertising method for a product depends on the target market and the company budget. Who is the company trying to reach? How much money does the company have to spend? The company will seek the highest number of target customers at the most affordable cost.

While researching advertising options, the features of each will be considered. For example, a television commercial is very expensive, and there is a limited time to show and tell the viewer about the product. A magazine advertisement is less costly, yet it is just a picture without movement. Internet advertising has the challenge of trying to catch a viewers attention among many pictures and products. A radio commercial is a moderate cost for advertising, yet does not show product images, and listeners can easily ignore radio commercials. Direct mail includes postcards, letters, and catalogs in the mail. Often these items are seen as unimportant when they arrive in a mailbox. A billboard is not expensive, but since drivers go by quickly, the message is usually only able to be a few words and one picture. Temporary signage is the least costly and is also the least effective. Temporary signs can be easily damaged by weather and can be viewed as a less professional type of marketing.

THE COST OF MARKETING

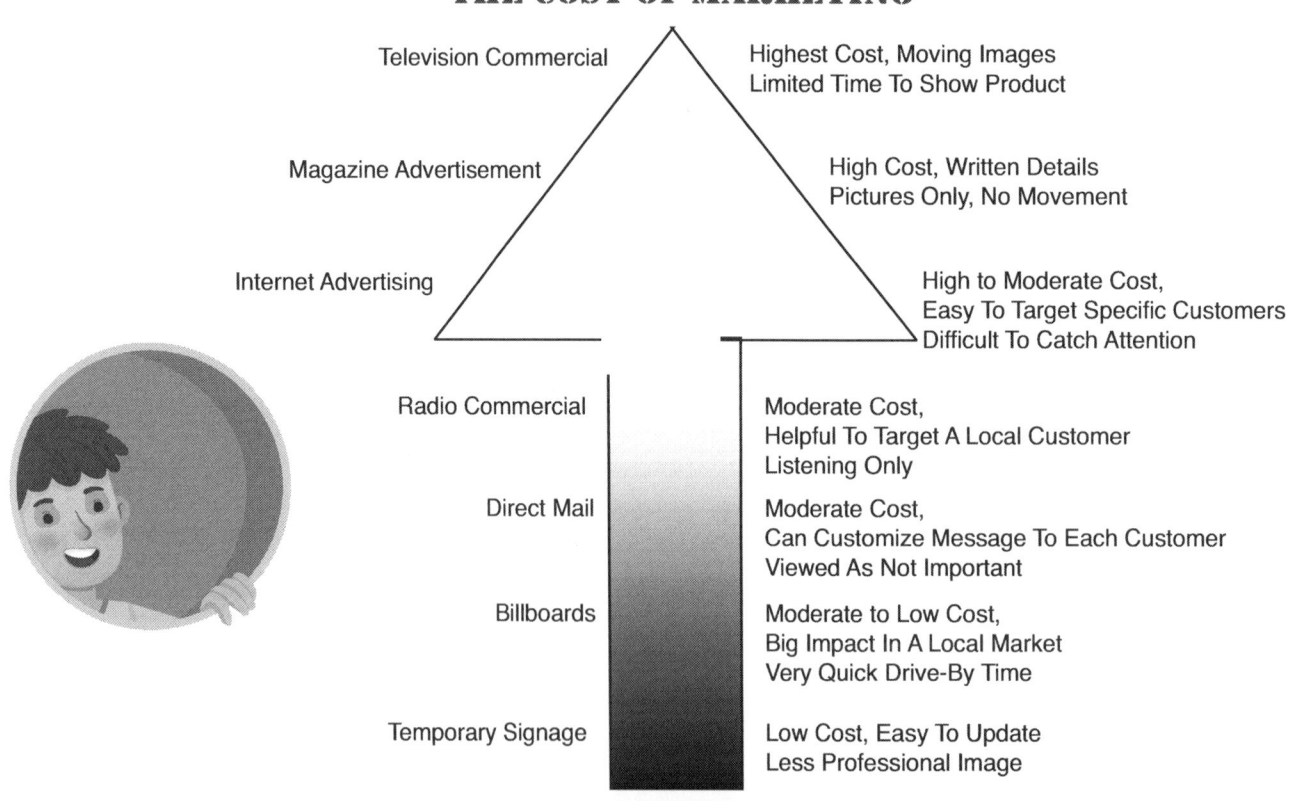

Television Commercial	Highest Cost, Moving Images, Limited Time To Show Product
Magazine Advertisement	High Cost, Written Details, Pictures Only, No Movement
Internet Advertising	High to Moderate Cost, Easy To Target Specific Customers, Difficult To Catch Attention
Radio Commercial	Moderate Cost, Helpful To Target A Local Customer, Listening Only
Direct Mail	Moderate Cost, Can Customize Message To Each Customer, Viewed As Not Important
Billboards	Moderate to Low Cost, Big Impact In A Local Market, Very Quick Drive-By Time
Temporary Signage	Low Cost, Easy To Update, Less Professional Image

The Drawing Board

Commercial TV

Select your favorite toy or hobby. Imagine a company that sells the toy contacted you to ask for a new idea for a commercial. Below is a storyboard for a commercial that will be 30 seconds in length. Each square in the series represents 5 seconds in the commercial. First, sketch a picture of what is happening in the scene. Next, write a few words in the box to describe the scene.

What is the product? _____

Who is the target market for this product? _____

CREATE

Marketing Math

How does a company keep track of the number of products it sells? How does a company know if a marketing plan has been successful? When does a company know it is time to add more products? When is the correct time to raise a price? Or is it time to stop selling a product? Each of these questions can be answered with math.

A company typically has an accounting department. Accounting will keep records of the sales and expenses for a business. The accounting department will also have a history of the sales results for the products that are sold. To keep track of the business sales a company may use a simple sales statement to show the results of business activities.

After a few years of operations a company will have a history of sales statements. Looking at the financial statements over time will help the marketing team identify trends. The trends studied may be about the cost to make products or the growth or decline of company sales. Understanding past trends help a manager make more accurate predictions about future results. If there is a pattern that shows a sales increase each year a company will likely request more products to sell. But, if there is a decrease from year to year, a company may choose to lower a product price. The company may also decide the product has entered the life cycle exit stage and no longer sell the item.

The Wayve Surf Shop Company
Simple Sales Statement
01/01/2019 - 12/31/2019

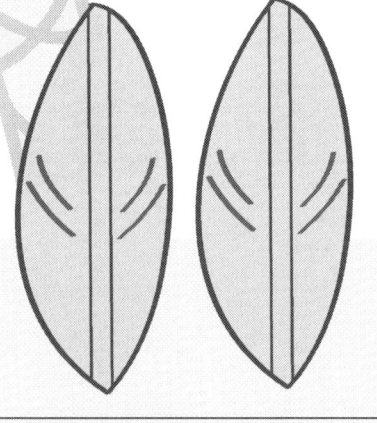

Gross Sales	$82,000
Less: Returns	$ 2,500
Less: Sales/Discounts/Coupons	$ 9,000
Net Sales	$70,500
Less: Cost of Goods Sold	$25,500
Less: Operating Expenses	$42,400
Net Income	$ 2,600

The Drawing Board

The Sales Statement

Refer to the Simple Sales Statement for Wayve Surf Shop and answer the following questions in the space provided.

1. What is the total amount of gross company sales at Wayve Surf Shop? _____

2. What is the total amount of net sales after the returns and discounts? _____

3. The cost of goods sold is the total amount the company had to spend to have the product available to sell. This would include surfboards, suntan lotion, bathing suits, and all the other products for sale in the store. How much did the company spend on products to sell between January 1, 2019, and December 31, 2019?

4. The operating expenses are the total amount of money the company spent to keep the business open. This would include electric bills, rent, employee paychecks, government taxes and display racks. (This does not include any product that is sold.) How much did the company spend to operate, or run, its business in 2018?

After the company paid all the bills, the money that remains is called profit. The profit is the money when there are no bills currently due to be paid. The profit of a business may be used for several purposes. A business goal is to grow. The profit that is in the bank after all costs are paid can be used by the business to grow and expand. Updates to a business may include product updates, hiring new employees, developing an existing marketing program, or updating employee uniforms.

5. How do you think Wayve Surf Shop may choose to invest the profit?

6. The average sale at Wayve Surf Shop is $110. Using this information, along with the gross sales figure form the Simple Sales Statement, approximately how many sales transactions did the company have in 2019?

7. The company has two employees, each paid the same amount. Payroll is included in the operating expenses total. At the surf shop payroll is equal to 50% of the operating expenses. What did one employee earn in payroll during 2019?

COMPUTE

Sale! Sale! Sale!

Have you noticed signs in a store to let customers know the store is having a sale? "Everything 20% Off" and similar signs tell a customer that is product is being offered at a lower price. A company offers a sale for two main reasons:

      (1) To encourage new customers to visit a store

      (2) To sell products that are not selling as quick as the company planned

A sale provides a customer with a chance to save money on items. At the same time a sale gives a company an opportunity to sell slow-moving merchandise.

In the market there is competition for just about every product. A company usually focuses on one of four different approaches to compete for customers.

    1. By Offering Low Prices - *Price*
    2. By Providing Excellent Customer Service - *Place*
    3. By Selling Unique Items - *Product*
    4. By Having Rewarding Discount Clubs - *Promotion*

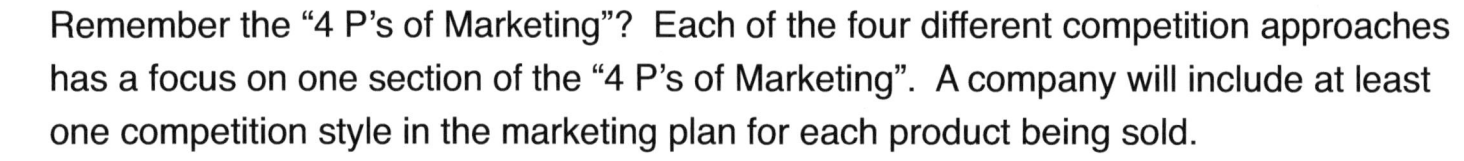

Remember the "4 P's of Marketing"? Each of the four different competition approaches has a focus on one section of the "4 P's of Marketing". A company will include at least one competition style in the marketing plan for each product being sold.

How To Change A Decimal To A Percent

Step 1: What number do you want to change to a percent?

Step 2: A percent is a part of 100. If you ate 49 jellybeans and the bag had 100 jellybeans then you ate $\frac{49}{100}$ or 49% or .49 of the jellybeans in the bag. To make a decimal a percent move the decimal two places to the right. The decimal .49 will become the percent 49%. $\quad \frac{49}{100} = 49\% = .49$

Step 3: In some cases the original decimal will have more than two digits in the number (example: .875). In this case when you change the decimal to a percent the answer will have a decimal. (example: 87.5%)

Step 4: If the answer needs to be rounded to a whole number the standard rounding rules apply. If the number to the right of what is being rounded is 4 and lower the digit stays the same. If the number to the right is 5 and higher the digit being rounded will be moved up one digit higher. (example: 87.5% rounds to 88%)

The Drawing Board

Find The Sale Price

Pet-A-Torium, Inc. is celebrating 20 years in business and as a thank you to customers the store is having a big sale! Compute the sale prices below.

Pet-A-Torium

Celebrating 20 Years Of **Woof**-Tastic Customers! We **Tank** You. **Fin**-ish Your Day At Our Store. You Will **Meow** At The Sale Prices!

Show Your Work in This Column

1. Product: *Kitten Toys*
Current Price: $5.00
Sale Discount: 40 %
Sale Price: $ 3.00

(1) Change percent to decimal 40$ = .4
(2) Multiply $5.00 x .4 = $2.00 to know sale discount
(3) Subtract the full price from the sale discount
    $5.00 - $2.00 = $3.00
$3.00 is the sale price for the kitten toys.

---

2. Product: *Hamster Food*
Current Price: $7.99
Sale Discount: 10 %
Sale Price: $

---

3. Product: *Rabbit Hutch*
Current Price: $85.00
Sale Discount: 25 %
Sale Price: $

---

4. Product: *Puppy Beds*
Current Price: $19.95
Sale Discount: 30 %
Sale Price: $

---

5. Product: *Bird Cages*
Current Price: $59.95
Sale Discount: 20 %
Sale Price: $

COMPUTE

Copyright Protected.

How To Read A Budget

Wayve Surf Shop Company	2018 Budget	2018 Actual	**2018 Variance**	2019 Budget
Revenue				
Gross Sales Revenue	69,000	70,100	2,100	75,500
Less: Returns	200	400	400	500
Net Sales Revenue	68,800	70,500	1,700	75,000
Expenses				
Advertising	8,000	8,500	(500)	9,000
Electric	3,000	3,200	(200)	3,400
Inventory	25,500	25,500	0	23,500
Office Supplies	3,500	3,600	(100)	3,800
Payroll	21,200	21,200	0	28,000
Repairs	4,000	4,200	(200)	1,000
Telephone	1,700	1,700	0	1,700
Total Expenses	65,900	67,900	2,000	70,400
Net Income	2,900	2,600	(300)	4,600

- In 2017 the best guess for 2018 results.
- The actual 2018 sales and expenses.
- The difference between the best guess and actual.
- In 2018 the best guess for 2019 results.

What is Revenue? - Revenue is the amount of money a company makes selling products. Gross revenue is the product sales *before* any returns or discounts are deducted (taken out) from the total. Net revenue is the actual sales amount, *after* customer returns, coupons and discounts are deducted from the total gross sales amount.

What is a Variance? - A variance is the difference between two numbers found by subtracting. Example: Wayve Surf Company repairs are budgeted at $4,000. The actual costs for 2018 were $4,200. The variance between the numbers shows the company overspent by $200.

What is Net Income? - Net income is the amount of money a company has earned after the costs to run the business are paid. Costs related to doing business include the amount needed to have a marketplace where customers can buy products.

What is the ( ) before and after a number shown in the variance column? - When a company spends more money than the budget planned a variance column would show " ( ) ". The numbers in the parenthesis show how much money was overspent by category. For example, Wayve Surf Company spent an extra $500 than budgeted for advertising shown as (500).

Note: The negative symbol, " - ", may be used in place of " ( )"

The Drawing Board

Word Problems

Answer the questions below in the space provided using the information shown in the budget on the previous page for Wayve Surf Shop.

1. Wayve Surf Shop Company has decided to budget $75,500 in net sales for 2019. Looking at the budget data, is this a reasonable goal? Explain your answer.

2. In what three categories did the company spend the same amount as the budget?

3. Is the 2018 to 2019 net income for the company expected to increase or decrease?

4. What two categories are planned to be the largest expenses in 2019?

5. (a) What is the total amount spent on inventory in 2018? _____
   (b) What are the total net sales in 2018? _____
   (c) Using the answers from a and b: How much money did the company earn in sales above what they paid for the inventory (known as the mark-up)?

6. Bonus: The repairs in 2018 were $4,200. The amount the company plans to spend is in the budget for 2019 is $1,000. What do you think is a possible reason why the 2019 budget is below the 2018 actual spending results?

COMPUTE

Y.M.B.A. Marketing Review

Congratulations on completing the Y.M.B.A. Marketing learning workbook. Consider the questions below to demonstrate all you have learned. Write your answers on page 65.

1. A business that does a task for a customer is providing a:

    (A) Favor (B) Service (C) Trade (D) Good

2. The goal of marketing is to let customers know about:

    (A) Expenses (B) Sales results (C) Current events (D) Products

3. New product marketing is when a product is:

    (A) Re-stocked (B) Delivered (C) New to a buyer (D) New to a product line

4. A product may fail when introduced to the market due to all the following except:

    (A) Poor name (B) High price (C) Time of day (D) Poor idea

5. The simple formula to determine company profit is [Sales - _____ = Profit]

    (A) Months (B) Expenses (C) Units sold (D) Returns

6. A company may need to update its product when:

    (A) Competitor changes a design (B) The stock is low (C) The month ends

7. A new technology is most likely to affect products in which industry:

    (A) Electronics (B) Banking (C) Travel (D) Childcare

8. A competitor to ABC company offers very similar _____ to ABC company.

    (A) Locations (B) Receipts (C) Products (D) Parking

9. When marketing refers to a "product" it means:

    (A) Only a good (B) A good or a service (C) Only a service (D) Profit

10. When buyer habits for a product change there may be an increase in:
    (A) Demand   (B) Shelf space   (C) Return rate   (D) Expenses

11. When a product is purchased a customer expects it to:
    (A) Be free   (B) Work as advertised   (C) Have extra parts   (D) Be overpriced

12. Two book stores on Main Street in the same town are:
    (A) Direct competitors   (B) Co-workers   (C) Partners   (D) Consumers

13. A fruit stand and a grocery store are examples of:
    (A) Farming   (B) Eating healthy   (C) Indirect competition   (D) Trade

14. Which of the following is not a part of the "4 P's of marketing":
    (A) Product   (B) Price   (C) Place   (D) Profit

15. When you purchase something tangible did you buy a:
    (A) Stock   (B) Good   (C) Service   (D) Business

16. A toy factory makes a product and then most likely sells it to:
    (A) Friends   (B) Competitors   (C) Neighbors   (D) Distributors

17. An example of a marketplace is a:
    (A) Outlet mall   (B) Website   (C) Retail store   (D) A, B, and C

18. Prices ending in which numbers appear more appealing to customers?
    (A) 5 and 9   (B) 4 and 8   (C) 0 and 7   (D) 2 and 6

19. Which of the four below is the best marketing price for an ice cream?
    (A) $1.05   (B) $0.95   (C) $1.00   (D) $0.94

20. A picture or design that customers recognize as part of a company is a:
    (A) Product   (B) Drawing   (C) Image   (D) Logo

21. The abbreviation "PR" is for the marketing term:
    (A) Price ratio   (B) Per retail   (C) Public relations   (D) Pay rate

22. Knowing your customer in marketing is called:
    (A) Introductions   (B) Data   (C) Demographics   (D) Information

23. Your favorite designer just came out with a new style shirt that you:
    (A) Need   (B) Want   (C) Both A and B   (D) Wait for a sale

24. A town has lost the electric and a company donates food is an example of:
    (A) Public relations   (B) Promotion   (C) Sales   (D) Competition

25. AIDA help summarize marketing steps. The first "A" is to get a customers
    (A) Activity   (B) Action   (C) Attention   (D) Approval

26. Customers no longer want a product, in which life cycle stage is the product?
    (A) Introduction   (B) Maximum   (C) Minimizing   (D) Exit

27. A company would prefer to have a product stay in which life cycle stage:
    (A) Moving   (B) Maximum   (C) Minimizing   (D) Exit

28. A survey asks, "Do you like strawberry yogurt?" is what type of question?
    (A) Friendly   (B) Open-ended   (C) Professional   (D) Closed

29. A focus group gathers data from:
    (A) People   (B) Books   (C) Computers   (D) Products

30. A commercial shows a person stuck in a rainstorm. This is ____ marketing.
    (A) High fashion   (B) Envy   (C) Fear   (D) Ability

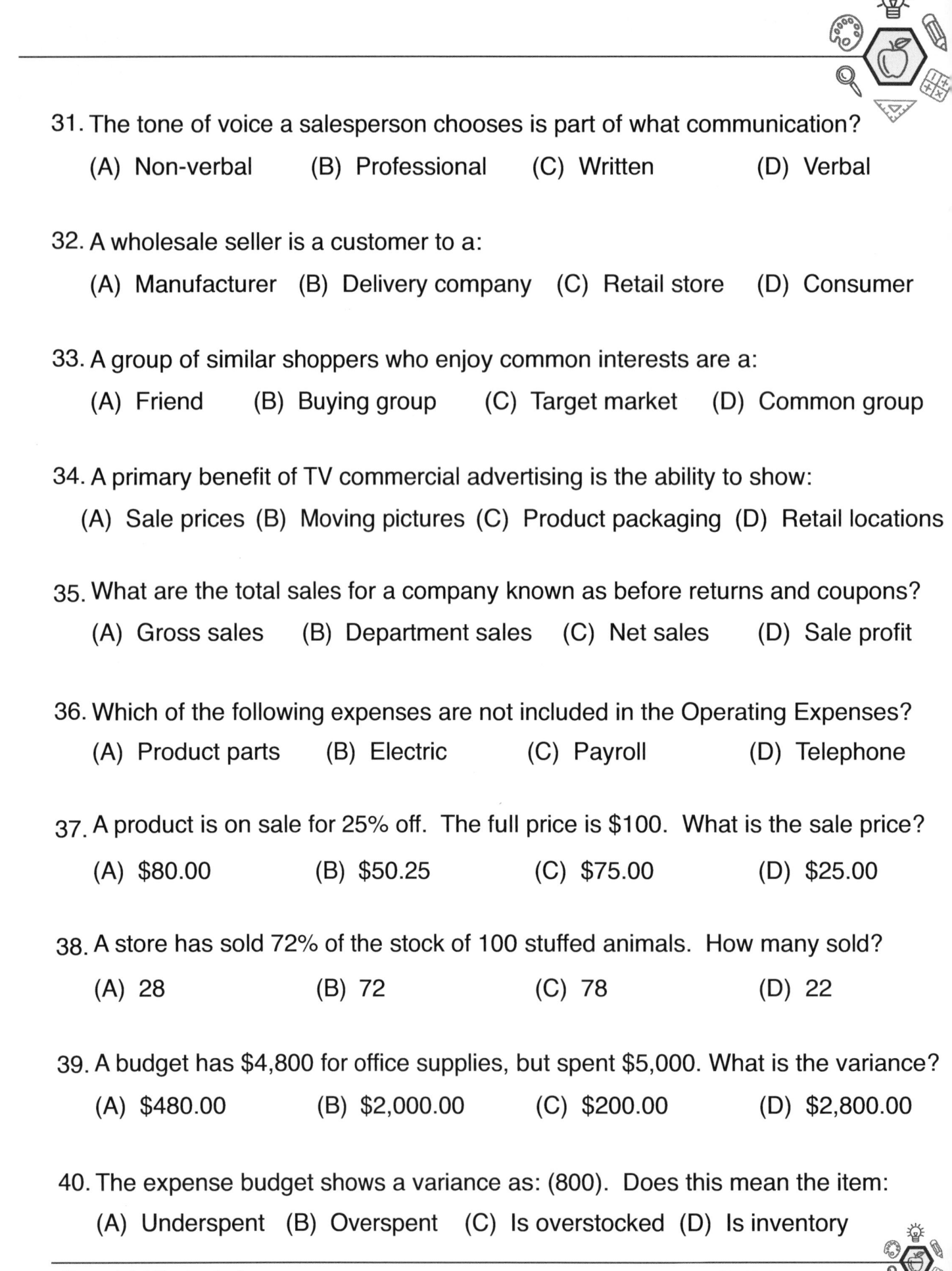

31. The tone of voice a salesperson chooses is part of what communication?

    (A) Non-verbal   (B) Professional   (C) Written   (D) Verbal

32. A wholesale seller is a customer to a:

    (A) Manufacturer (B) Delivery company (C) Retail store (D) Consumer

33. A group of similar shoppers who enjoy common interests are a:

    (A) Friend   (B) Buying group   (C) Target market   (D) Common group

34. A primary benefit of TV commercial advertising is the ability to show:

    (A) Sale prices (B) Moving pictures (C) Product packaging (D) Retail locations

35. What are the total sales for a company known as before returns and coupons?

    (A) Gross sales   (B) Department sales   (C) Net sales   (D) Sale profit

36. Which of the following expenses are not included in the Operating Expenses?

    (A) Product parts   (B) Electric   (C) Payroll   (D) Telephone

37. A product is on sale for 25% off. The full price is $100. What is the sale price?

    (A) $80.00   (B) $50.25   (C) $75.00   (D) $25.00

38. A store has sold 72% of the stock of 100 stuffed animals. How many sold?

    (A) 28   (B) 72   (C) 78   (D) 22

39. A budget has $4,800 for office supplies, but spent $5,000. What is the variance?

    (A) $480.00   (B) $2,000.00   (C) $200.00   (D) $2,800.00

40. The expense budget shows a variance as: (800). Does this mean the item:

    (A) Underspent (B) Overspent (C) Is overstocked (D) Is inventory

Y.M.B.A. Marketing Review Student Test Sheet

Congratulations on your completion of the Y.M.B.A. learning workbook. Enter your answers in the spaces provided below.

1. _____
2. _____
3. _____
4. _____
5. _____
6. _____
7. _____
8. _____
9. _____
10. _____

11. _____
12. _____
13. _____
14. _____
15. _____
16. _____
17. _____
18. _____
19. _____
20. _____

21. _____
22. _____
23. _____
24. _____
25. _____
26. _____
27. _____
28. _____
29. _____
30. _____

31. _____
32. _____
33. _____
34. _____
35. _____
36. _____
37. _____
38. _____
39. _____
40. _____

This page intentionally left blank.

Y.M.B.A. Drawing Board Worksheet Answer Key

Page 8: answers will vary.
Page 9: answers will vary.
Page 10: (1) various, may include sale or discount offer (2) answers will vary.
Page 11: answers will vary but should contain promotion, place, price, product name.
Page 12: answers will vary.
Page 13: answers will vary.
Page 14: answers will vary, name should include details so the buyer knows what it does.
Page 15: answers should work together to form a consistent marketing message and idea.
Page 16: details should have a poor name choice, high price or a poor concept idea.
Page 17: (1) poor name (2) poor idea (3) high price and poor name (4) poor name (5) poor idea (6) answers should include either poor name, high price or a poor general idea.
Page 19: answers should include a positive feature of the product update or addition.
Page 21: each of the eight items at the top of the page should be included on one of the eight lines at the bottom of the page.
Page 23: answers vary,
Page 25: (1) good (2) both (3) service (4) good (5) good (6) both (7) good (8) both (9) both (10) service
Page 27: (1) customer will pass full price items on the way to the clearance racks. (2) answers will vary but should bring the women's and children's close in spaces next to each other.
Page 29: box front should have a picture of the clock, a name of the product, a price and some features.
Page 31: (1) $0.75 (2) $4.95 (3) $0.99 (4) $0.95 (5) $0.49 (6) $4.95 (7) $0.99 (8) $0.75 (9) $0.89 (10) $5.55 (11) answers will vary (12) answers will vary (13) higher prices will appear lower when ending in 5 or 9.

Page 33 Top: (1) answers should include various charity functions or services. (2) answers will vary but should include a promotion or gift of appreciation. (3) answers vary, may include fast response or lending equipment or tools. (4) answers should include tools that keep the name present such as a baseball team sponsorship, a billboard, free t-shirt give away.
Page 33 Bottom: (1) to (10) answers will vary but should include company brand names.
Page 35: (1) Circle: water, medicine, bar of soap, place to live. Underline: puppy dog, bottled water, scented shampoo, notebook with sparkle, designer medicine case, video game. (2) many shoppers would buy the luxury soap since a little more money, but an extra bar and extra quality. (3) urgent (4) urgent (5) time to shop (6) time to shop.
Page 37: Answers should include: (1) an attention grabbing phrase or word (2) a promotion or limited sale would keep the buyer interest (3) rare or useful features would create buyer desire (4) a limited time or limited stock creates action.
Page 39: (1) answers will vary. (2) technology and competition cause changes in the market. (3) Unlikely due to high demand, no coupons needed to convince shoppers to buy. (4) Less demand will cause the price to go down. (5) answers will vary. (6) minimizing (7) moving, growing stage. (8) introduction entrance stage
Page 41: (1) leading (2) non-leading (3) non-leading (4) leading (5) closed (6) open (6) closed (7) open
Page 43: (1) good (2) good (3) good (4) good (5) service (6) service (7) good (8) service. Product examples sold will vary.

Page 45: answers will vary.
Page 47: (1) preparing food, bringing food the table, cleaning your table. (2) 84 (3) the large part of the business is repairing items, a service. Parts are only sold as part of the service. (4) sharks are a scary tour, need to build buyer confidence in tour guides.
Page 49:

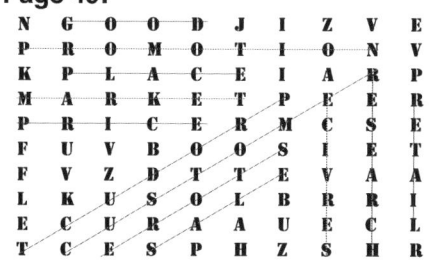

N	G	O	O	D	J	I	Z	V	E
P	R	O	M	O	T	I	O	N	V
K	P	L	A	C	E	I	A	R	P
M	A	R	K	E	T	P	E	E	R
P	R	I	C	E	R	M	C	S	E
F	U	V	B	O	S	I	E	T	
F	V	Z	D	T	T	E	V	A	T
L	K	U	S	O	L	B	R	R	I
E	C	U	R	A	U	E	C	L	
T	C	E	S	P	H	Z	S	H	R

(1) retail (2) market (3) place (4) price (5) sale
Page 51:

Two-2-Go Baby Stroller — Target Market: Age 20-40, Location: National, Interest: New Parents
Fitness Restore Health Water — Target Market: Age 20-40, Female, Location: National, Interest: Team Sports
Fresh Sports Flower Scented Bags — Target Market: Age 20-40, Location: National, Interest: Fitness
Pet360 Handy Vacuum — Target Market: Age 40-60, Location: National, Interest: Crafts
Ciz-Or Fabric Cutters — Target Market: Age 20-40 and 40-60, Location: North USA, Interest: Winter Sports
365 Solar Sun Glasses — Target Market: Age 20-40 and 40-60, Location: National, Interest: Animals
Rugged Turf Snow Boots — Target Market: Age 15-30 and 20-40, Location: South USA, Interest: Outdoors

Page 53: answers will vary.
Page 55: (1) $82,000 (2) $70,500 (3) $25,500 (4) $42,400 (5) answers will vary (6) $82,000 divided by 110 = 745 customers (7) $42,400 divided by 2 since payroll is half expenses = $21,200. Next, $21,200 divided by 2 since two employees = $10,600 each
Page 57: (1) $3.00 (2) $7.19 (3) $63.75 (4) $13.96 (5) $47.96
Page 59: (1) Yes, sales numbers show a small increase each year (2) payroll, inventory, telephone (3) increase (4) inventory, payroll (5) (a) $25,500 (b) $70,500 (c) $70,500 - $25,500 = $45,000 (6) various answers about a known repair at the end of 2013 that was planned to be made in 2014.

Y.M.B.A. Marketing Review Answer Key

1. B
2. D
3. D
4. C
5. B
6. A
7. A
8. C
9. B
10. A

11. B
12. A
13. C
14. D
15. B
16. D
17. D
18. A
19. B
20. D

21. C
22. C
23. B
24. A
25. C
26. D
27. B
28. D
29. A
30. C

31. D
32. A
33. C
34. B
35. A
36. A
37. C
38. B
39. C
40. B

Certificate of Completion

Presented To

_____

Upon Successful Completion of the
Youth Master of Business Administration
MARKETING

Presented By _____

Date _____

© www.YMBAgroup.com

Y.M.B.A. Single Topic Learning Workbooks

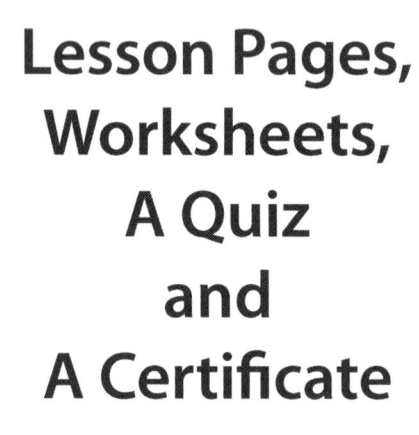

Lesson Pages, Worksheets, A Quiz and A Certificate

Learn Life Skills & Business with Y.M.B.A.

Benefit from 100 top tips and tricks that will enhance the effectiveness and enjoyment of your internet-based virtual classroom presented by virtual teacher, recruiter and trainer, L.J. Keller. A must-have book for anyone considering, or currently teaching, English virtually as a second language! Benefit from ideas, techniques and examples for English lanugage learners. These easy to implement concepts can enhance your classroom and effectively increase your students comprehension. Students also enjoy learning in this active learner classroom environment. Ideas are presented with clarity using examples that can provide you with a competitive advantage in the virtual classroom. Enjoy this all-in-one solution to help you launch and sustain amazing student results.

Are you ready to be an amazing virtual teacher?

Ready to define your S.P.A.C.E.?
Do you know your 4 E's?

www.YMBAgroup.com

ISBN 9781690614036

Do you know someone who would like to work from home?
Virtual teaching is a wonderful option!
Work from home.
Flexible schedules.
Amazing students!

This one book can help you quickly achieve a successful virtual classroom.

100 Tips are ready to assist!

Recruiting for virtual teachers with a four year college degree, any major at:
www.YMBAgroup.com

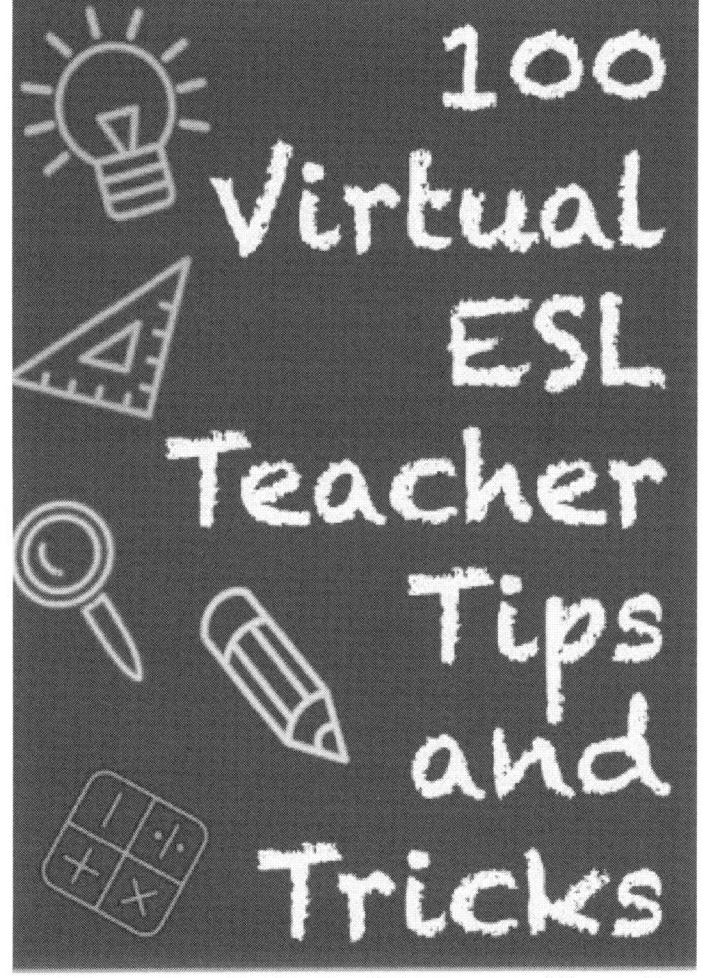

100 Virtual ESL Teacher Tips and Tricks

Proven Ideas For Student Enjoyment and Success!

L.J. Keller, M.B.A.

SPLASH: A waterpark mystery

Moore Mysteries Book 1

The champion is part of a secret plan! Solve the mystery as you meet Battle, twins Rachel and Reese, Zack and Morgan as they travel the United States with their parents. In this first book in the series the family begins a road trip adventure. The first *family fun stop* finds a mystery the family works together to solve. Join the family as they race to tell the judges. What was the secret plan? How will the kids find the judges to stop the results in time? What is discovered?
Grades 2-4/Ages 6-8/Early Chapter Book

Look Inside!

Skill Builder practice and a Book Quiz Included

**Engaging Reading Books
plus
Skill Builders & a Book Quiz
An easy way to demonstrate
learning accomplishments.**

Chapter Books That Are Fun To Read and Include A Quiz To Demonstrate Completion

57 Days: Miriam Short Sails With William Penn

YMBA Days In History Series

Learning Book Quiz Included!

Join Miriam, Adam and Anne Mary, on their journey from England to America with William Penn to see the land he was granted in the New World by the King of England. Exciting history based on actual people and events. Experience the triumphs, struggles, loss and dreams while traveling across the Atlantic Ocean to a new home. Discover the path so many experienced as they left their home for America. Details vividly paint a picture of the conditions on the ship and the difficult days along the way.
What challenges did they endure?
What were the fears and hopes of the young adults?
An exciting historical adventure of the journey to America.
Join Miriam on her voyage with her family and William Penn.
GRADES 6-10/AGES 11-15/ FACTION CHAPTER BOOK

Available on AMAZON.com and retail sites such as BarnesandNoble.com

Printed by Amazon Italia Logistica S.r.l.
Torrazza Piemonte (TO), Italy